Statistical Deception at Work

Statistical Deception at Work

by
John Mauro

LEA **LAWRENCE ERLBAUM ASSOCIATES, PUBLISHERS**
1992 Hillsdale, New Jersey   Hove and London

Lawrence Erlbaum Associates, Inc., Publishers
365 Broadway
Hillsdale, New Jersey 07642

Library of Congress Cataloging-in-Publication Data

Mauro, John B.
    Statistical deception at work / John B. Mauro.
        p.   cm. — (Communication textbook series.   Journalism)
    Includes bibliographical references and index.
    ISBN 0-8058-1232-6 (p)
    1. Social sciences—Statistical methods.   I. Title.   II. Series.
HA29.M296   1992
001.4′22—dc20   92-6753
                                                                       CIP

Printed in the United States of America
10   9   8   7   6   5   4   3   2

Contents

Preface

Statistical thinking will one day be as necessary for efficient citizenship as the ability to read and write.

— H. G. Wells

That "one day" is today. If you cannot understand simple statistics, you can be fooled by news stories, advertisements, and daily encounters with other people. You are likely to be taken in by modern-day medicine men who are out there seeking ways to dupe unsuspecting journalists into becoming their agents.

There are many people dealing with numbers from the wrong side. Television commercials and print advertisements have been doing it for years: "20% fewer cavities." Twenty percent fewer than what? Teeth? People? How did they come by that number?

Reports from public opinion pollsters and the mass media's own polls are regular features of many newspapers, magazines, and television news programs throughout the country. Nowadays reporters don't interview people; they take polls.

One reporter covering the end of a bus drivers' strike in a

large city, who rode on the first bus to begin operating, wrote this. She said, "An informal poll of bus passengers showed that most of them had paid friends to drive them to work during the forty-three-day lapse in bus service." There were 16 passengers on the bus and the time was 4:55 a.m.

These days, when you ask a person on the street for directions, you haven't asked a person, you have conducted a randomly selected interview. Ask two people and you will have conducted an "informal survey." Ask three people and you have done a "scientific survey."

All too often how we report numbers is influenced more by circumstance and desire than by objectivity. For example, we often see television audience figures appearing in newspapers. Television Station A sees a profit in sharing its numbers. It reports total late-night television audience viewing share as shown here.

Station A	50%
Station B	31%
Station C	19%

The implication here is that there is 100% television viewing. In reality, only 16% of the population said they watched late-night television. As you see here, the percentages representing the persons watching late-night television were substantially lower.

Station A	8%
Station B	5%
Station C	3%

From the station's point of view, 50% looks much better than 8%. What they neglected to mention was that 16% was the base of the share percentages.

Averages can be as ambiguous. Ever hear this one? "I have one foot on a bed of hot coals and one foot on a cake of ice. On the average, I feel fine."

Averages are trickier than that, however. For example, on my block there are 22 houses. One family that spends winters in Florida lives in a house valued at $450,000. The son-in-law, who lives next door and works for the family, has a house worth $400,000. There is a banker, an automobile salesman, and an advertising agency account executive, and each has a house valued at $250,000. There are four houses worth $125,000 each. There are five houses estimated at $100,000 each, and eight houses each having values of $70,000.

I don't mind telling you that I live on a block where the average house is worth $144,000. Or is it $100,000? Or is it $70,000? Each of these averages is correct. I have three choices regarding the affluence with which I am associated: upper, middle, or low. If I am thinking of selling my house, I shall choose the high average. If I am talking to a real estate tax assessor, I shall choose the low average. In yet other cases, the median ($100,000) is the best describer of the value of my street.

How does this happen? Well, there are several methods of calculating an average. I have selected the three methods that are used often. Later I describe how each average is calculated.

Public opinion polls are popular these days. Some independent pollsters publish their findings through syndicated columns, whereas major mass media companies make news by reporting findings of their public opinion polls.

Their reports are quick to point out the sampling tolerance of a particular poll (i.e., plus or minus these many or those many percentage points). By admitting there is a small leeway in the precision of the numbers, they give the impression that the poll is cleansed of all bias. They say little about the wording of questions, and they seldom publish them.

Here is an illustration of how a bias can enter a question. Recently a major media company reported that 67% of the adults in a national study said that abortions should be allowed. The question was:

"If a woman wants to have an abortion and her doctor agrees to it, should she be allowed to have an abortion, or not?"

The way the question is worded, the public is answering more on the issue of freedom of choice of the mother than on the issue of abortion. The imprimatur by the doctor, a respected medical expert, which provides the assurance that there is no medical danger to the mother, adds to the bias. Had the question alluded to the killing of a fetus, approval might have been much lower.

So choose your weapon. A woman's right will get you one answer, killing an unborn child will get you another.

Although reporters are required to confirm news accounts, they are not required to verify numbers or the methods by which the numbers are generated. If educated journalists are taken in, how can we expect the public not to be similarly fooled? People tend to believe what they get from news media, particularly if the stories use numbers. There seems to be a sort of mysticism to numbers among many people. As a consequence, it is crucial that reporters have a clear understanding of numbers and how they should be interpreted so that, by reporting them, they in turn do not extend false numeric evidence to their audiences.

For example, recently a newspaper ran a story about a study conducted by two university ornithologists who predicted, from the study, that cats may be responsible for killing up to 26 million songbirds in the state. The study quantified other small animals killed by the survey cats.

The study was conducted during the first 11 months of 1990 among five cats: four in a suburban county living with one researcher and one cat in a rural county living with the other researcher.

The behavior of five cats was used to project the killing of up to 26 million songbirds in the state. This is like predicting peanut butter consumption in the state from the consumption behavior of my six children.

Do you think that five cats constitute a representative sample of cats in the state? No!

Were the cats selected by a statistically sound sampling procedure? No!

Were the projections valid? No! (Although the researchers acknowledged that the "statewide bird-kill estimates are rough at best.")

If the reporter or the editor of the newspaper had asked the researchers these three questions, do you think the story would have run?

Where is the credibility of the story? Well, cats do kill birds and other small animals. We know that already. How would this story mislead the public? Some people who dislike cats may take drastic action against neighborhood cats as a result of reading the story, particularly because the story quoted one of the researchers who provided such a stimulus by saying, "How long can our native (animal) populations withstand such pressure from this one factor alone?"

The following pages go more into the topics just mentioned and the fooling around that goes on with index numbers, charts and graphs, correlation, convenient numbers, and more.

This book views numbers from a public perspective and illustrates how the naivete of journalists often nourishes quantitative misinformation. It is intended to make you, the journalist, a more critical appraiser of the numbers thrust at you every day. To be naive about the meaning of numbers is to be a carrier of misinformation to thousands of persons who read or listen to your news stories.

Averages: Ambiguous in Assorted Ways

Averages are used to describe a set of numbers that, by themselves, would be difficult to comprehend. We are exposed to averages every day. We see averages of rainfall, incomes, outside temperatures, wind velocity, heights of people, prices, and averages of many other statistics. Put in the wrong hands, they can be as misleading as a mirage.

BASEBALL'S BATTING AVERAGE

In baseball, a batting average is a handy device for getting a quick idea of the likelihood that a batter will get a hit. The announcer might say that the player's batting average is 250. Translated, this means that this batter has an average of getting a hit once out of four times at bat. It is calculated by getting a tally of the number of hits and dividing it by the total number of times at bat.

If this player has batted 400 times and during the same period has had 100 hits, his batting average is .250. Instead of dealing with decimals, baseball officials multiply batting averages by one thousand to make the number more easily understood. Imagine if this arithmetic device was not available. We would have to try to get some understanding of a batter's performance by reviewing 400 records.

Kinds of Averages

There are several common kinds of averages:

Arithmetic Mean
Median
Mode
Geometric Mean, and
Harmonic Mean

The geometric mean and the harmonic mean are used with certain data usually not encountered by the general population. Therefore, we shall not bother with these averages. The arithmetic mean is the average we are most used to seeing and has many uses. The median is less popular but it is used often. The mode is the average most used by mass media, usually when they interview "the person on the street."

The Arithmetic Mean

Calculating the arithmetic mean is straightforward and simple. It is accomplished by adding all the values in a set and dividing by the number of values. Averages are calculated in the manner shown in Table 1.1 for a set of ten numbers.

The Median

To calculate the median, it is necessary to arrange these numbers in ascending or descending order. Let's put them in ascending order (Table 1.2). The median is 3.5. It is the middle value. There are an equal number of values above and below the median.

TABLE 1.1
Arithmetic Mean of Ten Numbers

3
2
5
3
6
9
3
4
9
3
47 ÷ 10 = 4.7 = Mean

TABLE 1.2
Median and Mode of Ten Numbers

2	
3	
3	
3	← 3 = Mode
3	
	← 3.5 = Median
4	
5	
6	
9	
9	

The Mode

Once the numbers are listed in order, we also see that the mode is 3. This is the number appearing most often. The mode is often a category most often mentioned, or a particular response given most often. To calculate the mode, count the frequency of appearance.

Mean, Median, and Mode: All Averages

Much to the delight of some, the *mean, median,* and *mode* are all averages and may be referred to by their common term. However, the arithmetic mean is generally referred to as the average. The median is generally reported as a median, but one hardly sees or hears the term mode. It is usually identified in textbooks. Outside of the academic world, the mode is most often used without identification.

Now let's see how these averages work in depicting the affluence on my block mentioned previously in the Introduction. (See Table 1.3.)

The Average Value of Houses on My Block is $144,000. The total value of the 22 houses on my block is $3,160,000. This sum divided by 22 produces an average (arithmetic mean) house value of $143,636 which rounds to

TABLE 1.3
Housing Values on My Block (In Descending Order)

$ 450,000	
400,000	
250,000	
250,000	
250,000	
125,000	
125,000	
125,000	
125,000	
100,000	
100,000	
	← $100,000 = Median
100,000	
100,000	
100,000	
70,000	
70,000	
70,000	
70,000	← $70,000 = Mode
70,000	
70,000	
70,000	
70,000	

$3,160,000 ÷ 22 = $143,636 = Mean

$144,000. That is the average value. If I want to impress a prospective buyer, I shall use this average.

The Average Value of Houses on My Block is $100,000.
The median housing value is $100,000. There is an equal number of values above and below $100,000. In this example, there are eleven values above and eleven values below the median. Generally, the median is used when a few items in the data set are extremely high or low, causing a large dispersion among the numbers to be averaged.

The Average Value of Houses on My Block Is $70,000.
The mode is the value that appears most often. In the case of the housing values on my block, there are more houses valued at $70,000 than any other price. If I were talking to a tax assessor or applying for financial aid, I would use the mode as the average to represent the affluence of my block.

By judicially selecting the appropriate average, I can create a desirable numerical atmosphere — desirable for me, that is. Of course, when I do this, it is a judicious use of an average. When an opponent does it, however, it is a devious manipulation of data.

PERSON-ON-THE-STREET AVERAGE

Mass communication media sometimes do a notable job with the mode. They have translated this term to mean "the person on the street." The answer given most often by these few people is translated as the answer from the public in general. Often we hear and see the statements "American say," "New Yorkers say," "Texans say." They are misleading indeed.

Effects of Dispersion on the Arithmetic Mean

The average of 1 and 99 is 50, $(1 + 99) \div 2 = 50$. The average of 49 and 51 is also 50, $(49 + 51) \div 2 = 50$. The number 50 does little to describe 1 and 99 because there is considerable dispersion between the numbers. The average does a superior job of describing 49 and 50 because there is so little dispersion between the numbers. To say that the average of 7, 10, 13, 16, or 199 is 49 is misleading. The median, 13, provides a more accurate description of the data. Statisticians call these unusually high or low numbers in a set "outliers" and sometimes disregard them when calculating averages or other statistical parameters. In this case, 199 is an outlier because it is substantially greater than the other four numbers in the set.

Average Deviation, Better Known as Standard Deviation

The standard deviation of a set of numbers, for practical purposes, is an average deviation of the numbers from their arithmetic mean. Since the total of the deviations from the mean equals zero, the average deviation must be calculated in another manner. Consequently, it is called standard deviation. You need not know how to calculate the standard deviation to use it. For example, the standard deviation of 1 and 99 from their average of 50 is 49, while the standard deviation of 49 and 51 from their average of 50 is 1. Clearly, the average having the smaller standard deviation more accurately describes the data.

Increase Dispersion to Bamboozle

Employers can do a classic job of bamboozling employees. The employer sees a way to use averages to make himself look like an employee benefactor. He boasts that he has increased his payroll by 11% while the inflation rate is 6% and business has been flat. He is generous beyond description, so he says.

What he gave his 50 employees was a 5% increase in salary. However, he gave his wife, to whom he pays $200,000 per year, a 30% increase. He gave his two sons, who receive a $100,000 per year salary each, and his cousin, who gets $50,000 per year, a 20% increase in pay. Including the other 50 employees, he gave $160,000 in salary increases from a payroll of $1,450,000 or an average of 11% (160,000 ÷ 1,450,000 = .11 or 11%). Eleven percent looks much more generous than five percent.

When an Average Gets You Half

The odds on winning a state lottery are basically averages except that we know in advance that the average is one. The average is one — one out of many possibilities. The odds of accurately picking three numbers from 0 to 9 are 1 in 1,000. The odds of picking 6 numbers from 0 to 44 are 1 in 7,059,052. Few persons ever calculate the odds (averages). If they did calculate them, they likely would not play the game. States never pay off according to the odds. If they did, they wouldn't make any money. Usually the winner's payoff is about one-half of the amount specified by the odds. If a person continually plays a state lottery, he is destined to lose. The consolation to the winners, for not getting all that they should, and to all the losers, is that this money goes to pay for schools, roads, hospitals, fire fighting, etc. Can you think of any loftier purposes?

Who Is Included?

We know well that poor people are more inclined to look for the pot of gold at the end of the rainbow. They are more inclined (and can least afford) to play state lotteries. These are not words lottery operators care to hear. Therefore, any data published by lottery entrepreneurs usually is "couched" in some way. The image they try to create is that money taken in by a lottery comes mostly from the well-to-do persons who can easily afford it.

Recently, one state published data showing that the average person in the high-income group spent substantially more money playing the weekly lottery than did the average player in the low-income group. On the surface, this data looks quite innocent. The rich can well afford to gamble. Upon analysis of the data that was used to calculate the averages, one sees that, taking into account a player's income, the average player in the low-income class spent proportionately more than five times as much of his income on weekly lottery tickets than the average player in the high-income group. Thus, when the data is available, one can dig out the truth about an average. Alas! That is not the case most of the time. Those who fear criticism will find many reasons for not providing enough information for you to make an intelligent appraisal.

THE AVERAGE AMERICAN

The most popular average of all is the number attributed to the "average" American, the average man or woman, or the average family. These numbers abound and we are exposed to them almost every day. The average American is exposed to this many advertising messages per day, or takes that many taxi rides in a month, or drinks so many bottles of gin in a year. Do you ever wonder how these numbers are obtained? Look into it some time, or read Chapter 6.

SUMMARY

The arithmetic mean is the average most frequently used. It also can be the most misleading because its value is affected by a wide dispersion of the data. Extreme low or high values within the data set can have significant effect on the resulting average as illustrated earlier in this chapter.

The median eliminates the effects of wide dispersion. However, it uses only the mid-value of the data ignoring dispersion entirely. As a consequence, it is difficult to judge its precision. The median is usually used with data that has no upper limit, such as personal income.

The mode requires only observation of the value or category in the data set that appears most often. It is most useful when there are few values in the data set that provide only one modal subset. It is a ready-made parameter for the person-on-the-street interviews commonly used by mass media.

WHAT YOU CAN DO

If the data comes to you from a press release, ask the supplier how the average was calculated. Ask to see the standard deviation. If this is given to you, simply divide the standard deviation by the average. Multiply the quotient by 100 to convert it to a percentage. Statisticians call this percentage the coefficient of variation or the coefficient of dispersion. If it turns out that the coefficient is 100% or more, you will know that the set of numbers have a wide dispersion, indicating that the average is not a good descriptor of the data.

If the standard deviation is not available, ask to see the minimum and maximum values. At least you will see the spread within the data and that ought to give you an idea how closely the average describes it.

The Test of Reason

Averages in the hands of a manipulator can be devastatingly misleading. A deceiver has the option of selecting the average to use. He can conceal data in one instance and include it in another as our "generous" employer did.

We seldom see the numbers used to compute the averages that are thrust upon us. If we could see such data, we could make an intelligent appraisal. Because we usually cannot see the data, we must use reason to protect ourselves from being fooled. We must ask ourselves if the average quoted is reasonable—that is to say, does it make sense? Is it possible to have extremely high or low values in the data that may mess up the average? For example, if someone were to tell us that the average salary in his company is $70,000 per year, we should need to know what occupations are included. If the chief executive officer's and other top executives' salaries are included, then it is not too difficult to imagine the wide dispersion in the data. That average would be a poor indicator of the salaries in that company.

Averages that may have wide dispersion of values are income, volume, distance, speed, and so on. Averages of data that do not have extreme upper or lower limits usually can be trusted. Average heights of American men or women are likely to be trusted. If a person was to tell you that the average height of the men in his neighborhood is 6 feet, 5 inches, you probably would not believe him. Outside temperatures in the United States, for example, are not likely to average 135 degrees. We are often exposed to that kind of absurd data. As a result, we should make reasonable judgments about their validity.

Who Gains?

Finally, ask yourself the purpose of being exposed to this average? What will the supplier gain from making it public? Question it seriously, particularly when an overly ambitious, super public-relations person is trying to convince you to publish his release. If you choose not to question such numbers, then I have a car the sale of which I should like to publicize. Trust me. The cars I sell are on the road an average of 11 years. But, if you do question, and you don't like the answer, don't run the story. You will do your audience a big favor by not running it. If your editor insists that you run the story, you'll know that soon you will have his job.

Percentages: Machiavellian Misleaders

At a dinner one evening recently, a man announced that those who deal in numbers are bean counters. He asserted with pride that he didn't know anything about numbers and cared even less about them. In response, his employer, who was sitting at the table, said that he was glad to know this because starting the next day, his salary would be cut by 50%. Because he didn't know anything about numbers, he should be just as happy with his new salary. If you profess not to know anything about numbers, you are a ready-made target for the percentage scam. Niccoló Machiavelli, a medieval Florentine scoundrel, likely would have used the same logic as the employer.

COMPARISON OF NUMBERS MORE EASILY UNDERSTOOD

Generally, percentages are used to reduce two or more large numbers into smaller ones. For example, a story in the newspaper reporting on a shareholders meeting stated: "That

proposal was defeated by a wide margin — 13,911,317 shares
in favor versus 631,354,999 shares against, or 2.2% versus
97.8%. . . ." The percentages make the comparison more
easily understood. In doing so, one number is given the value
of 100 and thus becomes the divisor. Accordingly, the other
numbers used to compare become the dividends. Therefore,
percentages convert ratios or fractions from large numbers
having many digits into two- or three-digit whole numbers
that are more easily understood. As we shall see, we pay a
stiff price for the simplification that percentages provide.

Any number, large or small, that becomes the base of a
percentage takes on the value of 100. One over 2 becomes
50%. One thousand over 2,000 also becomes 50%. Therefore, 50% of 2 is 1 and, accordingly, 50% of 2,000 is 1,000.

Win by Switching the Base

You can do yourself proud by giving your employee a 10%
pay increase and equally giving yourself a 10% increase. You
can assert with pride that you did not give yourself any more
than you gave your employee. Lovely! What you avoid
saying is that your employee's salary is $30,000 per year and
your salary is $120,000 per year. As a result of this shifty
maneuver, you take home an additional $12,000 per year,
whereas your employee takes home $3,000 per year more. By
shifting the base from $30,000 to $120,000, you cleverly
concealed that you have given yourself $9,000 more in the
pay increase than you gave your employee. Scrooge will love
you for this deed.

To Be Compared, Percentages Must Grow
from a Similar Size Pot

A story recently appearing in a newspaper headlined, "Retailers are feeling catalog, TV shopping." An expert (university professor) was quoted as saying, "The growth rate of
catalog sales alone is double that of retail sales." (The growth

rate is usually stated as a percentage difference of the current year over the previous year. Last year's figure takes on the value of 100.) The implication here is that catalog sales are threatening retail sales. What the story didn't say is that store sales are ten times that of catalog sales.

Hypothetically, if catalog sales increased by 10% per year and store retailers' sales increased by 5% per year, it would take 50 years for the catalog sales to catch up to store sales, assuming that the growth rates remain unchanged during the next 50 years. Historically, catalog sales have not improved their position significantly in relation to retail sales. Another fact not mentioned in the story was that many large store retailers also have catalog sales.

Another news story using the same numerical interpretation ran this headline: "Fewer married, more divorced." That headline was based on the percentage of divorces going up and the percentage of marriages going down. During the same period, there were twice as many marriages as there were divorces. The marriage rate was down from 10.5 marriages per 1,000 people to 10.2 marriages per 1,000 people. The divorce rate was up from 4.9 divorces per 1,000 people to 5 per 1,000 people. Clearly, there are more married, fewer divorced.

Don't Be Fooled by Arithmetic Done to Percentages of Independent Occurrences

Sometimes we are exposed to the absurd use of percentages. A television weather reporter recently announced that, "There is a 50% chance of rain on Saturday and a 50% chance of rain on Sunday." Therefore he concluded, "There's a 100% chance of rain over Saturday and Sunday." The chances of rain on Saturday and Sunday are independent occurrences. Therefore, the two percentages cannot be treated arithmetically. If you don't think this is absurd, then try this. Add the percentage chance of your favorite race horse winning for as many consecutive races it loses until --

TABLE 2.1
Percent Chance of Your Horse Winning

First race	10%
Second race	20
Third race	5
Fourth rate	40
Fifth race	25
Total	100%

reach 100%. For example, if your horse loses several consecutive races as depicted in Table 2.1, bet all you own on that horse in the sixth race.

According to this logic, your horse cannot lose. It has a 100% chance of winning the sixth race. Tell your friends to bet all they have on the same horse. After the race is over, head for the hills or, as luck might have it, and you need to celebrate, come to my restaurant. I'll give you a 40% discount on the celebration dinner. Bring a friend along. I'll take 20% off your friend's bill and 20% off your bill.

Greater / Smaller than What?

Here is another use of the "shifty" percentage. My brother is 9% taller than I am, but I am only 8% shorter than he is. If being short is undesirable, when my brother speaks, he uses 9%. When I speak, I use 8%. We are both correct. The difference comes from using a different base to calculate each percentage. My brother is 6 feet tall. I am 5½ feet tall. The difference between our heights is 6 inches or .5 feet. The percentage difference taken from 6 feet as the base calculates to 8%. The percentage difference taken from 5.5 feet comes to 9%. When the difference between the original numbers is large, we can expect to see an equally large difference in the percentages. If I were only 4 feet tall, then I can say that my brother is 50% taller than I am, $(6 - 4 = 2) \div 4 = .5 = 50\%$. On the other hand, I can say that I am 33% shorter than my brother, $(6 - 4 = 2) \div 6 = .33 = 33\%$.

Base Follows "Than"

When considering calculating the percentage difference between two numbers, which number should you use? In principle, it is the number to be used to make the comparison. When I say I am 8% shorter than my brother, I am relating the difference to his height. When I say that my brother is 9% taller than I am, I am relating the difference to my height. Usually, the number used second in the statement or that which follows "than" is used as the base of the percentage. When we say that his book has 20% more pages *than* that book, the number of pages from "that book" takes on the value of 100%. In business we often hear that sales this year are "so many percents" greater than last year. Last year's sales are the base. Sometimes *over* is used instead of *than*. One might hear that sales this year increased so many percents over last year.

Advertisements Hardly Ever Make Valid Comparisons

We read and hear percentage difference used often by advertisers. It has become their custom never to use than or any other word that establishes a comparison. In their ads and commercials they say, for example, costs 30% less . . . or 80% less cholesterol . . . or 50% more value. Costs 30% less than what? Has 80% less cholesterol than what? Has 50% more value than what?

Watch Out for Percentages Drawn from Small Numbers

Percentages are handy devices for the self-styled Davids of this world to knock down their perceived Goliahs. This Lil' Ole Magazine boasts it has 33% more readers in the upper income group than that nasty Great Big Magazine. This is a pretty convincing statement coming from an advertising salesman from Lil' Ole Magazine. What this slick salesman didn't explain to his prospects is that Lil' Ole Magazine has a total of 100,000 readers, whereas Great Big Magazine has a total of 25,000,000 readers. Lil' Ole Magazine has 40% of its readers in the upper income group. Great Big Magazine has 30% of all its readers in the upper income group. The Lil' Ole Magazine advertising salesman calculated a percentage difference between the two percentages, $(40 - 30 = 10) \div 30 = .33$, or 33%.

Percentages Cannot Be Treated Arithmetically Unless They Are Drawn from the Same Base

There are two things wrong with the logic in the previous paragraph. First, 40% of Lil' Ole Magazine's 100,000 readers represents 40,000 readers in the upper income group, whereas 30% of the Great Big Magazine's 25,000,000 readers represents 7,500,000 readers in the upper income group. It is not too difficult now to detect which magazine has more readers in the upper income group.

Second, the Lil' Ole Magazine's salesman calculated a percentage of a percentage. This is not proper by anyone's standards. Percentages may be given arithmetic treatment only if they are derived from the same base number. To do otherwise is to compare tea with telephone poles.

Percents Versus Percentage Points

This brings us to the issue of the difference between percents and percentage points. As an example, let us say that Company A has a 10% share of market and Company B has a 15% share of market. Total shares for the market is 100%. Both Company A's percentage share and Company B's percentage share are calculated from the same market total.

Company A tells its stockholders that its share of market trails Company B by only 5%. Right? Wrong! Company A trails Company B by 50%. However, it trails Company B by 5 percentage points. When percentages are based on the same numbers as in this example, they can be looked upon as regular numbers. Then they are referred to as percentage points. The calculations are straightforward: $10 - 5 = 5$ percentage points; $(10 - 5 = 5) \div 10 = .5$, or 50%.

Misuse of Sampling Tolerance Percentages Often Misleads

Reporters, notably television newscasters, reporting on results of polls refer to sampling tolerance (covered in chapter 8) as plus or minus 3%, or 5%, for example. The term, percent, is used incorrectly. Sampling tolerances are calculated as percentage points. They mislead the public if used as percents. Plus or minus, say, 5 percentage points means that a response of 25% of the sample may fall between 20% and 30% if the entire population was queried $(25 - 5$ and $25 + 5)$. Taken as a percent, the response may fall between 23.75% and 26.25% $(.05 \times 25 = 1.25)$, $25 - 1.25$ and $25 + 1.25$, erroneously implying a greater precision than the sample warrants.

Omitting A Percentage Can Misinform

Sometimes the omission of a percentage can misinform. A television commercial sought contributions for research to conquer a disease that afflicts 5,000 Americans per year. If one considers the importance of eliminating any disease, affliction of one person is too many. However, we are discussing the non-use of percentages here, and 5,000 persons out of a total population of 248,000,000 comes to .002%. Had the commercial mentioned two-one thousandths of one percent, I doubt that this commercial would convince anyone.

THE 2% WHO GOT AWAY

Furor over the 1990 census undercount stemmed from municipal politicians, who saw the decline in their population as a reduction in federal assistance. The media made much about the 5.3 million persons the Census Bureau missed. Little or no mention was made about how this number stood against the total population. The census missed 2% of the 250 million people counted. It is impossible to count 100% of the population. The success or failure of a census count should be gauged as a rate (percentage) rather than an absolute number because, historically, the number of people to be counted next has been always higher than the census before. Except for 1980, all other censuses back to 1940 had larger undercounts than the 1990 census.

False Precision

Another ploy a foxy person uses to win an argument is to carry out a percentage to two decimal places. I knew a researcher who fooled people regularly with this ploy. He would say, for example, that 42.69% of the women under 40 years of age regularly wore miniskirts when dating older men. Hardly any one is likely to challenge the accuracy of such a statement. Carrying the percentage to two decimal places gives it an aura of precision. Try it some time. Make the statement understandably reasonable and see how many people challenge you. Remember, you too can be a scoundrel.

What to Look for

In evaluating percentages, a journalist always needs to know the base number from which the percentage is calculated. If the number from which a percentage is drawn is small or insignificant, it is likely that a percentage calculated from it will be high unless that number is equally insignificant. Conversely, it takes a much larger number to achieve a similar percentage value from a large base.

If 1% of a newspaper's readers read a story on bunion surgery, quite likely that 1% of the total audience might represent 95% of the readers who suffer from bunions. The reporter who wrote the story might chastise himself for achieving only 1% readership, but he would console himself by knowing that he reached 95% of those to whom the story was significant.

When two or more percentages are compared, the comparison can be meaningful only if the percentages are calculated from base numbers of similar size. As we have seen in the comparison of marriages and divorces earlier in this chapter, comparing percentages from different base numbers distorts the findings. This is a pitfall many reporters do not seem to avoid. It is just this kind of ploy that deceivers use to win arguments. There are those who deal in numbers who cannot distinguish between a percentage and a percentage point. There are those who know the difference and choose to use this knowledge to fool others.

Percentages calculated from the same base number may legitimately be given arithmetic treatment. When this happens, percentages become percentage points. To illustrate, let's suppose 10% and 12% have been calculated from the same base number. We can say that 12% is 2 percentage points more than 10%. We cannot say that 12% is 2% more that 10%; 12% is 20% more than 10%. However, if you feel compelled to lie to minimize the difference, you might say that 12% is only 2% higher than 10%. Try it some time. See how many people catch you.

SUMMARY

Percentages are useful in providing comparative information often needed in making decisions. For example, if 1,700 children seriously injured themselves in bicycles accidents, should this be reason enough for Congress to pass a law requiring all children to wear bicycle helmets? Hardly, because 1,700 represents a tiny percentage of all the children in the United States who ride bicycles. The number is not sufficiently large to *force* millions of bicycle-riding children to buy helmets.

Percentages transform all numbers large or small into 100. As we have seen, masterful deceptions can be perpetrated with this transformation. Always seek to learn the actual numbers that the percentages represent. You will avoid being fooled, and you may avoid deceiving your audience and make wiser personal decisions.

The Word Connection: Inflaters or Deflators

If you do not understand numbers, you are not likely to recognize certain words that make numbers appear to be what they are not. An obvious example of this is when a person says he is 72 years young. At the age of 72 years, one is not considered young. This statement does not refer to the old man's age. It refers to the state of his health. We are not puzzled by this statement because we know how to interpret it. We are also not tricked when someone refers to another as being only six feet, five inches tall. We have prior knowledge of how tall persons are likely to be. There are many instances, though, when we do not have prior knowledge.

NEGATIVES TAKE THE HIGH ROAD
POSITIVES TAKE THE LOW ROAD

Many people do not have prior knowledge of the United States economy and may be fooled by this headline: "U. S. economy sluggish, GNP [Gross National Product] report shows." Later in the story, it states: "In a report apt to raise recession fears, the Commerce Department said the Gross National Product, the broadest gauge of economic health, grew at a lackluster 1.7% annual rate in the spring quarter." Another stated that the "economy gains only 2%." The word, "only," is intended to indicate how little the economy grew. If you didn't know that an increase in the economy, or the Gross National Product, 1%, 2%, or 3% is about normal and desirable, you might begin to do some serious worrying about an impending recession.

If 1.7% is "lackluster" growth, it is a "plunge" in another instance. Another headline read, "Economic indicators plunge." Later in the story, we read that the plunge was 1.7%. If a decline of 1.7% is a plunge, what would a decline of 70% be called? Here again, the extent to which economic indicators move from month to month was not mentioned in the story. Ordinarily, economic indicators move up or down less than one percentage point. It might have been more truthful to have indicated the movement. It might have also been more truthful to state that the decline of 1.7% was not expected to continue, according to the experts. As expected, that rate of decline did not continue in subsequent months.

Smaller Percentages Spur Wilder Modifiers

It seems that, the smaller the percentage is, the wilder the modifying words become, depending on the perspective taken by the provider. For example, "Food prices soar . . . 1.2%." "New home sales plummet . . . 4.7%." Meanwhile, "Exports bring trade deficit down 15%." Good news doesn't seem to soar or skyrocket.

The Fascination with "Only" as the Big Deflator

Strategically placed, the word, "only," can be a great put-down. Try this on a well-educated person you would like to put down. Say, "So, you only attained a Ph.D?" Or, say to a rich person, "So, you have only $10 million, eh?" Or, to someone who has lent you money, say, "You expect me to pay back that measly $300 you lent me?" To a thin person who just told you that he weighted 125 pounds, you might respond "that much?"

An item appearing in a monthly newsletter stated, "Only

59% of the adults polled . . . talk with other family members during weeknights." Fifty-nine percent of anything is a majority. It should not be described as "only."

ANXIETY TO CREATE FEAR CONFUSES REPORTER

Here is a story written to create fear. However, the writer must have been turned around. The headline read, "Prices at wholesale plunge; decline biggest in three years." Reading that headline and the rest of the story, you would think there is real cause to worry. Decline in prices, whether at retail or at wholesale, usually is considered desirable to counteract inflation. In this case, the monthly decline was .4% (4/10 of 1%).

WHEN A CRASH IS NOT A CRASH

When the stock market "crashed" on Black Monday, October 19, 1987, The Dow Jones Industrial Average dropped 508 points, or 23%. A comparison was made with the similar day in 1929. On Black Tuesday, October 29, 1929, the Dow Jones Industrial Average dropped 13%. The comparison is not valid because the collapse of the stock market in 1929 started on September 3rd and continued through November 13th. Hysteria peaked on Black Tuesday that set in motion The Great Depression.

On Friday, October 13, 1989, big investors with seeming devilish intent celebrated the anniversary of the 1987 crash by selling off enough stock holdings to lower the Dow Jones Industrial Average by 191 points, or 7%. Stock market prices usually move in pennies a day, in increments of $\frac{1}{8}$ dollars or 12.5 cents. The Dow Jones Index and sometimes other indexes are structured to emphasize minute changes. That is why 191 points translates to 7%.

The point to be made here is that a decline of 23% usually is not a crash. Many businesses have survived after having a decline of that much or more. As it turned out, there was no prolonged decay of the stock market. Prices began to increase almost immediately.

Convincing Connectors

One can do a good job of convincing people when connecting certain words with numbers. For example, a commercial for a cracker cited that only 8 million people eat it. This number was compared to 18 million people who eat bagels, 85 million people who eat croissants, and 249 million people who eat white bread. The idea is that you could be one of this small exclusive group that happens to enjoy the good life. Look at it this way: Would you like to have this small, sophisticated group of 8 million people to your house for dinner?

Those who have the opposite tendency, usually when attempting to extract a contribution from you, may use the statement "as many as" 5,000 people suffer from certain agony. Your money is desperately needed for research to halt this pain. Viewing the number objectively, 5,000 is not a sufficient proportion of the 250,000,000 people in the United States to warrant national attention. But, if you are one of the 5,000 people affected, you may look at it differently.

WORDS TO WATCH

A few frequently used words and phrases to watch out for when reading or listening to numbers thrust at you.

Deflators: Only, meager growth, poor performance, mere, nose dive, tumbled, deteriorated, slipped, collapsed, disintegrated, toppled, shrank, as little as.

Inflaters: Astonishing growth, zoomed, skyrocketed, spiraled, shot up, lunged, as much as, as many as, bounced.

As you become more aware of the lexicon attached to numbers from data you are assigned to report on, no doubt, you will add many more words to the list.

SUMMARY

The point to be made in this chapter is that modifiers can distort numerical values. Modifiers can be downright liars. An unsuspecting person can be fooled or frightened in some instances by depressing numeric values with words. You must view number describers with cold detachment. If a 1% decrease is described as "whopping," you must decide if it is truly so. You should expect that the normal percent decrease must be substantially smaller than 1%.

Test How Well Word Connectors Work for You

Test word connectors on your friends: Never test them on your audience. The next time a friend asks to borrow $10 from you, just tell him that you would like to, but, unfortunately you have only $300 in your pocket and can't spare ten.

In addition, you can use superlatives to describe any numbers connected to you. You might say that you have a most desirable weight for your height. Just don't mention to whom it would be most desirable. You might say that you have near-perfect reading speed. If someone wants to test it, tell him that your pupils have just been dilated and you have vision problems at the moment, but you will be glad to test your reading speed at a later date. Try these ideas on several friends. See how long it takes to lose them.

Index Numbers:
The Concealers

Index numbers are based on the same principle as percentages. An index of 150 is obtained from the relationship 45 is to 30, or 1,200 is to 800, or 37,500,000 is to 25,000,000. As we shall see later, an unscrupulous person will conceal more than he reveals with index numbers.

USED TO SIMPLIFY COMPARISON

Index numbers usually are used to simplify a comparison between one number and another, or between one number and several other numbers. The number that is the basis of comparison takes on the value of 100 and thus it is called the base number or, simply, the *base*. The other numbers are compared to it. It is the logic used in establishing the base that causes concern.

Any Number Can Be a Base
Anyone can create a base number. For example, I shall make my height, 5.5 feet, the base for calculating index numbers. My wife's height is 5 feet, 2 inches, or 5.167 feet. Con-

structing an index with these two numbers, using my height as the base, is straightforward and simple. My height becomes the divisor. Therefore, 5.167 ÷ 5.5 = .94 × 100 = 94. If my wife's index was 100, her height would be equal to mine. Because it is 6 points less, we say that she is 6 percentage points shorter than I am. A friend is 6 feet, 6 inches, or 6.5 feet tall. Therefore, his index, based on my height, is 118 (6.5 ÷ 5.5 = 1.18 × 100 = 118).

The logic of using my height as the base has no merit. It makes sense only to me. If the index was based on the height of the average person, it would make much more sense. There are numerous indexes based on sound logic, and as many that make as little sense as my height.

Consumer Price Index

Probably the most popular index in The United States is the Consumer Price Index. It is used to measure the inflation rate at the consumer level. The Consumer Price Index is constructed by checking prices of all consumer goods and service purchases made by urban families. A representative sample of families in urban areas provides an initial list of goods and services in the quantities of, or the extent to which, the members of the sample purchase them. In turn, government researchers check the prices and the quantities, or the frequency, of those items at the suppliers or stores where the purchases are made. Quantities are multiplied by the current prices, resulting in consumption expenditures.

MAJOR CATEGORIES OF THE CONSUMER PRICE INDEX

In broad terms, the categories included are food and beverages, housing, apparel and upkeep, medical care, entertainment, and other goods and services. Other goods and services include tobacco products, personal care and expenses for education. Simply stated, anything one can spend money on is included.

Purchase Behavior Weights Changed
Every 10 Years

Although family purchase behavior is surveyed every decade or so, prices are checked monthly. The Consumer Price Index is calculated and reported each month for all goods and services combined and for several of its component categories, broad geographic areas, and some large cities. The index is calculated by weighting each component according to the amount spent for each. An average is derived from these numbers.

Currently the consumption expenditures for 1982, 1983, and 1984 are used as the basis for the weights. Thus, consumer prices at this period represent 100. Previously, 1967 consumption expenditures and prices were used in arriving at the base.

Fun with the Inflation Rate

Given that there are two reference dates, we can have a little fun with the rate of inflation. Table 4.1 shows the Consumer Price Index based on average consumer prices during the 1982–1984 period.

TABLE 4.1
Consumer Price Index This Year

(1982–1984 = 100.0)	
January	121.1
February	121.6
March	122.3
April	123.1
May	123.8
June	124.1
July	124.4
August	124.6
September	125.0
October	125.6
November	125.9
December	126.1

Looking at Table 4.1, we see that the index for January is 121.1. This indicates that the January consumer prices this year were 21.1% higher than consumer prices during the 1982–1984 period. During the next month, prices rose .5 percentage points, from 121.1 to 121.6. By the end of the year, prices had risen from 121.1 to 126.1, or 5 percentage points. This, then, is the inflation rate for this year according to 1982–1984 prices. However, to determine the inflation rate from the beginning of this year to the end of this year, what the media try to report, we must calculate what percent 5 percentage points is of 121.1 percentage points. When we do that, we learn that the inflation rate is 4.1%. As you can see, we have two inflation rates we can quote, 5 or 4.1.

Switch Base and Frighten the Innocent

There is another way to increase inflation substantially and, consequently, frighten the life out of a weak-hearted person. By shifting to the 1967 base, we have tripled inflation. Table 4.2 shows the Consumer Price Index numbers for the same

TABLE 4.2
Consumer Price Index This Year

	1982–1984 (100.0)	1967 (100.0)
January	121.1	398.0
February	121.6	399.6
March	122.3	401.9
April	123.1	404.5
May	123.8	406.8
June	124.1	407.8
July	124.4	408.8
August	124.6	409.5
September	125.0	410.8
October	125.6	412.8
November	125.9	413.7
December	126.1	414.4

prices This Year calculated using the two base periods. Prices were lower in 1967 than they were in 1982-84. As a consequence, the inflation rate appears accordingly greater.

The Media's Way of Switching Bases

Although the calculation for switching bases is straightforward, the mass media use an even simpler method of inflating inflation. When a monthly increase comes close to 1%, or is more than 1% higher than the previous month, you can be certain that they will predict double-digit inflation. This maneuver is accomplished by taking the difference between the previous month and the current month and multiplying it by 12. An increase of 1% will project to 12% over 12 months. The media assume that, for the next 12 months, the rate of price increases will remain the same; this hardly ever happens. As we shall see later in this chapter, mass media similarly predicts an impending recession when a month's decline in the Leading Economic Indicators Index is around 1%.

Value of CPI for Gauging Significance of Pay Raise

The Consumer Price Index can be a useful number to you personally. You may find it in any library by simply asking for it. For example, you can calculate where you stand in purchasing power every time your boss gives you an increase in pay.

Assume that the last time you received a pay increase was in January of this past year. Now it is January again and your boss gives you a 10% pay raise. Your salary then was, say, $50,000 per year. Now you make $55,000 per year. It is a good raise as raises go, but how much did you improve your purchasing power over last year?

Let us determine how much of a raise you really got. The Consumer Price Index last January, based on the 1982–1984 period, was 121.1. The current price index, on the same base period, is 126.1. By dividing the index now by the index then (not too difficult to do), we can determine how much of a real increase you received (126.1 − 121.1 = 5.0, 5.0 ÷ 121.1 = .041, .041 × 100 = 4.1%) − 4.1% inflation rate for this year. Inflation wiped out 4.1 percentage points of the 10% raise you received. This leaves you with 5.9% remaining above inflation − not a bad raise after all.

INDEX OF LEADING ECONOMIC INDICATORS

The index of Leading Economic Indicators is another number that the news media report each month. It is calculated and made public by the federal government. This index is intended to provide a forecast of the United States economy's performance for several months ahead. The index is comprised of 11 components or categories of economic activity that change ahead of the economy. Combined, they provide a short term forecast. A decline in the index suggests a slowing of the economy.

Table 4.3 gives you an idea of what the Index of Leading Indicators looks like for a recent 12-month period. The first column is the index. The second column is the percentage point change over the previous month, and the third column shows the percent change over the previous month.

One Month's Movement Is Not a Dependable Predictor

Often data for a few components arrives late. To meet the publication schedule, the index is calculated with preliminary data for the late components. When the final data is available for those components, the government publishes a revised index. By that time, it is too late. The media already has released their interpretation, usually based on the current month's index. You can see by the Table 4.3 that one must

TABLE 4.3
Index of Leading Economic Indicators This Year

	Index (1982 = 100.0)	Point Change	Percent Change
January	146.0	—	—
February	145.6	− .4	− .3%
March	144.7	− .9	− .6%
April	145.8	+ 1.1	+ .8%
May	144.2	− 1.6	− 1.1%
June	144.0	− .2	− .1%
July	144.1	+ .1	+ .1%
August	144.8	+ .7	+ .5%
September	145.0	+ .2	+ .1%
October	144.4	− .6	− .4%
November	144.5	+ .1	+ .1%
December	145.1	+ .6	+ .4%

look at several months to get an idea of the direction the economy is going.

If we were to judge the movement of the economy taking the months one at a time, we would have been sad in February and March; happy in April; sad in May and June; happy in July, August, and September; sad in October; and happy in November and December. It just may be too much drama for people with weak hearts.

Product Use Index

Advertising agency and advertising media people sometimes do fancy numerical footwork with a differently calculated index. Usually the index has to do with product usage. The percent of persons or households who buy a product in the United States or other broad geographic area is used as the base. Data of this kind are usually collected by sample survey methods. (There is more on this topic in Chapter 10.) Other geographic areas, such as cities, counties, or metropolitan areas are compared with the broad-area base. At other times, the product purchasing of the total population is used as the base and segments of the population are compared with it.

Small Bases Provide Wide Spreads

Advertising media sales persons like to compare product purchases with a base they call a *norm*. Usually a medium with a small audience likes to use index numbers of this kind. If an advertising medium has a very large audience, its index for any product type will not vary too far from the 100-base figure.

Reduce the Base Size, Win the Argument

An advertising medium having a small audience may find several products that its audience purchases at a high level. It never happens that if 20% of the population purchases aspirin in a given period, every fifth person purchases it. There may be 15 persons on one street, only two on the next street, and none on the street after that; when all the streets are added, it averages to 20. We can then say that the smaller a component or area is, the more likely it is that it will vary significantly from the average.

Let us say that 15% of the adults in America purchased a new automobile last year. In my neighborhood, 20% of the adults purchased a new automobile last year. Regarding the buying of new autos, my street has an index of 133, or is 33% higher than the nation ($20 \div 15 = 1.33 \times 100 = 133$). I live in an "automobile affluent" neighborhood. It makes little difference that I haven't bought a new car in 10 years. It is the neighborhood that counts.

Thirteen percent of the adults, in a mid-size southern market having 504,000 adults, purchased wallpaper last year. Fourteen percent of the market's Sunday newspaper adult readers bought wallpaper last year. Twenty percent of a local radio station's adult listening audience bought wallpaper last year. The station tells it this way: When it comes to reaching people who buy wallpaper, the station has the Sunday newspaper beat by a wide margin: Radio, 154; Sunday newspaper, 108.

The indexes are calculated this way:

$14 \div 13 = 1.08 \times 100 = 108$, the newspaper's index;
$20 \div 13 = 1.54 \times 100 = 154$, the radio station's index.

No mention is made that the newspaper has 425,000 readers, 14%, or 60,000, who bought wallpaper, whereas the station has 50,000 listeners, 20%, or 10,000, who bought wallpaper.

Fallacy of the Small-Base Logic

The fallacy of the radio station's logic is that an advertiser would have to buy advertising to reach wallpaper users in all the small audience media. Then he must select those that have higher-than-average wallpaper purchasers in their audiences. The likelihood is that there are as many small audience media that have fewer-than-average wallpaper purchasers. High-coverage media such as newspapers and general magazines never reach high indexes because their raw numbers represent a substantial portion of the total population. As a result, their audience reflects the overall status that represents 100 as the base. The data from Table 4.3, Index of Leading Economic Indicators, in this chapter, is a good example of this. There are about as many months with "up" numbers as there are months with "down" numbers.

SUMMARY

Like percentages, index numbers are often manipulated to show what the manipulator wants to show. Because the base number is made to equal 100, the real values are concealed. The logic for comparison is drawn from the values as they relate only to 100 similar to the logic of percentages.

What to Do

It is incumbent upon journalists to uncover the real meaning of the numbers. One way to uncover an index cover-up is to ask to see the base numbers. Another way is to apply simple logic. Virtually any base number from a city is smaller than that of a state. Base numbers from census tracts or zip code areas have to be smaller than those of cities. States, cities, counties and other community areas will have base numbers smaller than the United States. However, base numbers from individual small areas such as blocks, census tracts, or zip code areas often produce manifestly unstable indexes (extreme highs or lows).

Similarly, high-coverage media such as local newspapers have larger audiences than television or radio stations or magazines distributed in any given market. As a result, newspapers audiences produce more stable indexes than the other local media.

The danger lies when two index numbers having widely different base numbers are compared. As we have seen, indexes calculated from small base numbers will have larger fluctuations than those drawn from large base numbers. You can expect, for example, a census tract to have a very low index of, say, auto purchases one year and have a very high index the following year. It takes just a few automobile purchases to influence the index whereas it takes many purchases to influence the same index of a city, a state, or the nation.

5

The Fine Art of Fooling

If pictures are worth a thousand words, then clearly numbers translated into pictures by a deceiver can be just as effective. For example, if you have never met me or know how tall I am, I can fool you into thinking that I am much taller than I am. I do this simply by showing you an illustration (Fig. 5.1), in

FIG. 5.1.

this instance a silhouette, of me standing among other people who are substantially shorter than I am.

The one in the middle is me. I am five feet, six and one-half inches tall. I barely made it in the Marines. By comparison I look tall—tall enough to give you the wrong impression of my height. A friend recently said to me, "If you want to look young, hang around with older people." It is even easier to fool people with charts representing numbers because people hardly ever get to see the numbers before the charts are constructed. If you had seen me beforehand, I could not have fooled you with the previous illustration.

Illustrations Should Help Understand Numbers

Charts and graphs should make numbers more clearly understood by illustrating them in an artistic form. On the surface, this seems like a good idea, but don't let a designing person get hold of the figures first. He can illustrate those numbers so that few will look like many and many will look like few.

Here is a set of numbers representing last year's sales by months of a company, say, the Acme Hammer Company.

Stretch the Vertical Scale, Exaggerate the Variance

As its chief executive officer, you wish to see the monthly sales figures. Your production manager says that it is diffi-

TABLE 5.1
Monthly Sales of Acme Hammer Company
(In Millions of Units Last Year)

January	42	July	37
February	44	August	38
March	43	September	40
April	41	October	41
May	39	November	42
June	38	December	44

cult for him to assign work crews efficiently for steady year-round production. He claims that there is too much fluctuation in monthly sales. He blames the sales department. The production manager shows you Chart 5.1.

As you can see, Chart 5.1 clearly demonstrates sharp variance in monthly unit sales.

Flatten Vertical Scale, Minimize Variance

Typically, the sales manager vehemently denies such sales fluctuations. He implies that the production manager ought to visit a psychiatrist. According to his chart (Chart 5.2) there is hardly any variance in volume of monthly sales.

Obviously, we have here two managers with cheating hearts. Both managers distorted the data with their visualizations. The production manager set up a scale on the chart that magnifies the variance in monthly sales. He has you looking at the data as if it were through a microscope. Minute differences look extraordinarily large.

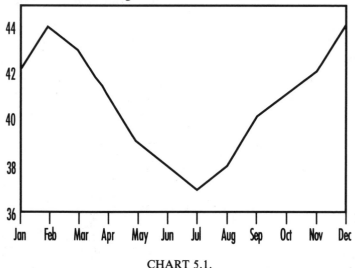

CHART 5.1.

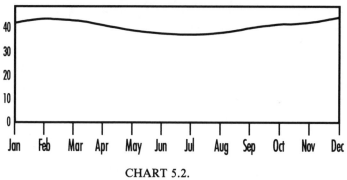

CHART 5.2.

Conversely, the sales manager sets the scale so that it appears to be in the distance as though you were looking at it from the other end of a telescope. As you can see, this minimizes the monthly variance in unit sales.

As an astute chief executive officer you are not easily fooled. You know that the conventional shape of a chart or a graph usually has a ratio of two values high to three values wide. You also know that the scale usually contains equal increments beginning at zero. Generally, both charts seem to meet these requirements. See how cleverly the production manager emphasized the variance. His scale goes from 36 million to 44 million, a range top and bottom of only 8 million units instead of 44 million units as it should be. Although the sales manager scales his data from zero, notice that the chart's dimensions are not in correct proportion. Its horizontal dimension is disproportionately larger, indicating a flat appearance.

These two managers are craftier than we think, but they can't fool you. That is why you are the boss. You know that, to determine if monthly sales vary significantly, you must compare them with another number. You know that it is not enough to say that something is higher or lower; higher or lower than what?

Average Variation

With this in mind, you summon your chief statistician, who probably constructed the charts for each manager in the first place. You don't ask him to construct a chart this time. Instead you ask him to calculate the average monthly variation in sales. In statistical jargon it is called *standard deviation*. Because this is an average variation, you compare it to the average monthly sales.

After having done this, you see that the average monthly sales vary by 2 million units. The average monthly sales are 41 million units. Thus the average variation is 5% of the average monthly sales. Knowing this, you can make the judgment knowing that your figurative leg isn't being pulled.

The Media Often Emphasize Small Variance

Newspapers, magazines and television news do a superb job of emphasizing variance between numbers. National unemployment percentages or inflation rates are ready-made figures for mass media ballooning.

Chart 5.3, which depicts unemployment rates, for example, is scaled in increments of one-tenth of one percent. An increase of six-tenths of one percent therefore looks much like a rocket shot. A decrease of a similar quantity looks like a nose dive.

You may become the victim of a visual double cross when you see charts like Chart 5.4.

To look at Chart 5.4 it would seem that the population "surged" ahead, whereas retail sales "plunged" during the past five years.

Vertical Scales Should Always Start at Zero

Correctly illustrated (Chart 5.5), it appears that neither the population nor retail sales moved much during the same five-year period.

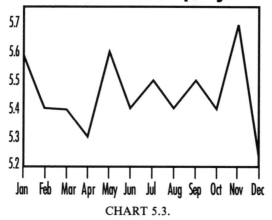

CHART 5.3.

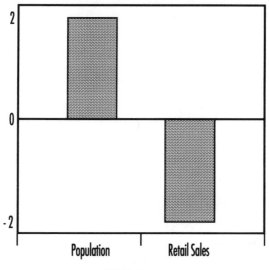

CHART 5.4.

Population-Retail Sales
Growth Last 5 Years

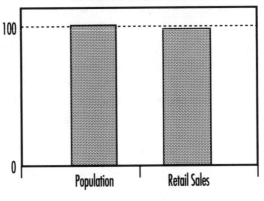

CHART 5.5.

USING AREA CHARTS TO DECEIVE

Another technique for a cunning deception is using the area of two objects to illustrate the difference in magnitude between two (or several) numbers. An unsavory salesman would use this method (Fig. 5.2) to show how superior his sales are compared to those of his competitor.

FIG. 5.2.

You see here that the automobile representing Dealer A is four times as large as the automobile representing Dealer B. When Company B complained, the crafty salesman from Company A said that all he did was to make the height of one car one-half as high as the other. "After all, that is how all bar charts are constructed," he said. He simply did just that. What he concealed was that reducing a photograph or an illustration by one dimension automatically reduces the other dimension by the same proportion. Pretty neat! He reduced the competitor's illustration to one-fourth the size, not one-half.

Double the Dimensions, Quadruple the Size

Sales of Company A appear to be four times the sales of Company B when they are only two times as much. Remember your high school geometry? The formula for calculating the area of a rectangle is the length times the width. When you divide the height by two, and you also divide the width by two, you divide the area by 2 × 2 or 4. If you don't believe me, look closely at some of the charts appearing in the mass media or ask a slick salesman.

Double-Cross With Maps

One can do a classic job of visual double-crossing by shading maps. States such as Colorado, Idaho, Montana, Utah, and Wyoming, known as the Rocky Mountain States, contain 3% of the people in the United States. Yet these people live in 14% of the area. Although "area" doesn't spend, eat, play, or do all the things people do, it's convenient to use it for comparisons.

According to the last United States Census of Population tiny Connecticut has over one million people more than Idaho, Montana, and Wyoming combined. Geographically, 65 states of Connecticut can fit into the area of those three states. How appealing the following map (Fig. 5.3) would

FIG. 5.3.

look to the Connecticut Chamber of Commerce. In population, Connecticut stands up like a Goliath among states.

The only thing in common that Connecticut has with the other states is that it is also classified as a state. Comparing statistics with the vast area of Alaska might be even more deceiving, but, alas, Alaska is not contiguous with the other states and visual deceptions using it would be easily detected.

SUMMARY

Charts whose values on the vertical scale do not begin at zero, or break the vertical scale just above the zero mark, or have large spaces between the scale increments are intended to emphasize the variance. Customarily charts are dimensioned two-parts high by three-parts wide. When charts are taller than they are wide, you can be sure that the intent is to exaggerate. It takes more care to detect distortion when illustrations are used. The size of the objects used may exaggerate the differences in the values being compared and sometimes may have no connection with the subject. Imagine how the area of Russia would compare with Monaco in casino receipts!

Lastly

Keep a critical eye on the data when you see it in visual form. Ask yourself the question: Is the chart or graph I am looking at representing the numbers honestly? Where are the numbers? Will I mislead the people to whom I will show this chart? Remember one can make an ape that is about the size of a human being look bigger than the Empire State Building. Messing up the meaning of numbers is much easier with illustrations.

6

Convenient Numbers: The Magicians

Hal Roach, the famous Irish comedian, tells the story about an Irish attendant who worked in a museum of natural history. One day a visitor, viewing the skeletal remains of a prehistoric dinosaur, asked him how old he thought those remains were. Without hesitation, the Irishman responded, "Three million and seventeen years." The tourist was amazed at the precision of the number and asked the Irishman how he came about such a precise figure. The Irish attendant explained, "Well sir, when I started working here they told me the dinosaur was three million years old, and I have been working here 17 years." Although the naiveté exemplified in this story is refreshing, calculations of similar convenient numbers are often made to impress, or to win an argument, or made out of sheer pomposity.

Here is an example. Two men are on a train traveling at 70 miles per hour across the countryside. One man sees a meadow full of sheep. He says to his colleague sitting next to him, "I wonder how many sheep are in the meadow we are passing." "Two thousand, one hundred and seventy-five," his colleague quickly responded. "That's extraordinary! How did you count so many sheep?" the man asked. "Oh," responded his colleague, "I didn't count the sheep. I counted the hoofs and divided by four."

Police Estimates of Crowds

The fastest counters have to be the police. They often are asked to tell the media how many people demonstrated, or watched a parade, or rioted. Typically the police provide such numbers, but because there is no way to verify them, they are accepted. Often several sources provide estimates of crowds and as often, the numbers vary as much as 100% between them. The police are used as the source to create an aura of honesty as well as precision (as though the police have extra God-given counting ability).

Estimates in Restricted Areas Less Difficult to Make

Usually when an event takes place in an arena or a similar enclosure where seats are provided, or admitting tickets are required, a more accurate count of the number attending is possible. It is less difficult to estimate the number of beans in a jar. With a little effort, one can calculate the volume of the jar and the average volume of a bean. The rest is simple arithmetic. Unlike beans in a jar, when an event is held outdoors and open to all, estimates of the number of persons attending abound. The size of the numbers vary depending on the motive of the estimator.

How Many Depends on the Estimator's Perspective

Recently, pro-life, anti-abortion, people rallied in Washington, D.C., against laws making abortions legal. They were told beforehand that they would have to muster 500,000 people to make a political impact. An Associated Press story reported that the United States Park Police estimated the crowd at 200,000 people at 4 p.m. Anti-abortionists quoted an estimate made by photographers who took photographs from the top of the Washington Monument at 2 p.m. They estimated the crowd at more than 500,000. If both estimates are correct, then 300,000 people left the scene in three hours. It is a wonder that no one was trampled on during such a massive exodus. When the pro-abortion people rallied a year earlier, estimates of persons attending ranged from 75,000 to 300,000.

PREPARATION HELPS

Disparities need not be so great. A little preparation will yield more precise estimates of crowds. For example, if a rally is planned on the grounds of the Washington Monument, the area of the grounds may be calculated from maps (if it is not available already). Measurements of a few people at standing position will provide the area generally taken up by one person. Let us say that the area of the grounds at the Washington Monument is 2,000,000 square feet. Space allotted to one person, measured and allowing for elbow room, is 3 square feet.

If the grounds are full at rally time, we can estimate 667,000 persons ($2,000,000 \div 3 = 666,667$). Aerial photographs, readily available from the police department, will indicate how full the grounds are and estimates may be altered accordingly. Although this technique provides crude estimates, it is significantly better than plain "eyeballing."

You can imagine someone looking over the crowd and, without hesitation, calling out a number. You may have done it yourself sometime. However, there are other numbers conveniently used, the flaws of which are not so easily detected. Those who use convenient numbers to deceive have two things in common. They never justify the logic they use and they never explain how the numbers they use are calculated.

The More Convenient a Number, the More Often it is Used

For years, top executives of advertising agencies quoted a universally convenient number for their industry. They often said that the average American was exposed to 1,500 advertising messages per day. It was such a convenient number that none of the persons who quoted the number felt compelled to verify it. When a top advertising agency executive made a sales presentation to acquire a prospective advertiser's account, this number worked like magic. With 1,500 messages competing daily for the consumer's attention, only his agency had the staff and know-how to produce the kinds of advertisements and media schedules that would stand out above the other 1,499 messages.

Unverified, Convenient Numbers Easily Debunked

Several years later, a young advertising agency researcher, probably having little respect for top executives, investigated the subject. He discovered that the average person was probably exposed to about one-fifth that number, or about 300 messages. Did the agency executives quit using that 1,500 number? You bet they did!

Not every contrived number can be exposed. Usually it takes too much effort to do so. It took the young researcher considerable effort to expose the 1,500 number. Because convenient numbers are difficult to verify, users get away with them.

Many Numbers Attributed to the Average American

The average American is the source of many convenient numbers. According to a television commercial, the average

American will have five automobile accidents in a lifetime. The implication is that every American will have five accidents. If you are seventy years old and have had no automobile accidents, you better brace yourself. You can be certain of avoiding them if you don't drive at all and you don't ride in someone else's car. If you drive and you are accustomed to taking passengers, you will be much safer if you take only those passengers who have had their share of all their five accidents. If you read Chapter 1, you will know that perhaps there is a reckless driving American who will have your share of accidents.

Convince by Switching Units

A foreign car manufacturer, in an attempt to illustrate how well-constructed its autos were, advertised these numbers.

The average American drives 45 years.

The average car is traded in every 3 years.

The average driver will own 15 cars.

Notice how the units are switched—from the average American to the average car to the average driver. Also notice how magically 3 and 15 multiply to 45.

The same auto maker emphasized that 95% of its cars registered in the past 11 years are still on the road. Why not? One car, owned by a driver who drove it to church only once a week, was registered 11 years ago whereas the balance of the cars still on the road could have been registered yesterday!

Expose Logic of Number

Sometimes it is not the number that needs to be exposed but the logic of it. The use of the per capita, or per household, or per "anything" often has extraordinary power to perform magic.

Years ago, the Census of Business reported retail sales for

political entities such as cities, counties, and metropolitan areas. Sales were credited to the political entity containing the store. The Census of Population reported the number of people and households in the same manner. What the Census Bureau didn't report was how many sales were made in a store by people who came from outside the area where the store was located. As a consequence, little Sioux Falls, South Dakota, ranked among the top ten cities in the nation in per-household retail sales. Calculation of this was straightforward. The total retail sales credited to stores in Sioux Falls, including purchases made by farmers and other people outside Sioux Falls, were divided by the total of only the people living in Sioux Falls. No one bothered to notice that, according to this calculation, people of Sioux Falls were spending substantially more money in retail stores than their total income.

Calculating a per number is simple. For example, the land area of the United States is 2,265,144,960 acres. There are 250,000,000 people in the United States. By dividing the acres by the people we get 9.06 acres per person.

Fair Share of Land Solves Major Social Problem

A social activist can have a field day with this number. The logic is that all Americans should own their fair share of land regardless of race, color or creed. Obviously the poor do not have their share, although the rich have more than their share. The situation is even more disgraceful, so they say, because poor people have more children and thus are entitled to have even more land. At 9 acres per person, a poor family of seven should be allotted 63 acres of land, whereas a rich family of three should be allotted only 27 acres. Carrying out this silly mathematical logic further suggests putting tight controls on population growth. Every time a child is born, each individual's allotted share of land is reduced accordingly. Conversely, everyone's share increases when someone dies.

Per Capita Does Wonders for the Rich and the Poor

The annual per capita personal tax is about $2,500. A poor family of seven would pay $17,500 in personal taxes; a rich family of three would pay only $7,500. It doesn't seem right, does it? Well, we can solve that problem. The per capita personal income is $17,000 per year. Thus, a poor family of seven would earn $119,000 and could well afford to pay the tax. Using the per logic, all it takes to get rich is to have many children. A family with many children would be allotted a sizable piece of land and would earn much money.

Numbers Pulled from the Sky

There is more. Convenient numbers spawn in many different ways. An article appearing in a newspaper told of a woman who attacked the tobacco industry. She said that 15% to 20% of the deaths in the state (Virginia) each year stem from tobacco-related illness. I wonder how she arrived at that figure. The percentage seems high when one considers that fewer than 4% of the deaths in the United States are caused by all chronic obstructive pulmonary diseases combined. It is hardly possible that Virginia's rate would vary so much above the United States. Perhaps this woman included smokers or tobacco company employees who died of boredom or who were shot by jealous spouses.

Any Number May Be Divided by Another Number

It is difficult to bamboozle a salesman. At an out-of-town weekend sales retreat, a comptroller cautioned the salespersons attending not to spend too much of the company's money. "After all," he said, "it takes $36,000 to open the door to the plant each day." He obviously arrived at this figure by dividing the total operating cost of the company by 365 days. A smart salesman forthrightly responded, "Each salesperson brings in $22,000 in sales per day. Have two salespersons open the door to the plant, and the company will make a profit just by opening its doors."

Off-The-Top Reasoning

Some accountants have a way of putting a damper on a business trip. They say that for every dollar you spend on the trip, it takes eight dollars of sales to make up for it. What they are saying is that the company is operating at a 12% profit. They try to fool you into thinking that the money you spend on the trip is coming off the top. Every operating expense supposedly comes off the top if a company expects to make 100% profit. It is impossible to do business without any expenses. Therefore, companies budget operating expenses against expected sales; very likely, all of your travel expenses have been budgeted in advance.

The Illogic of Comparing Unlike Parameters

Sometimes a convenient number user gets his numbers and logic crossed. A comic strip character answered this question: "Do wild turkeys get as big as the kind you buy in stores?"

The response was, "No . . . wild turkeys average about 17 lbs . . . the record domestic bird weighed over 63 lbs!" Notice the apple and orange comparison here. The response first compares a present size of wild turkeys to a past size of domestic turkeys. Then it compares an average weight, probably of many wild turkeys, with a single domestic turkey of extraordinary heavy weight. Comparisons between types or groups should be made of like parameters – average with average, extraordinarily heavy weight with extraordinarily heavy weight, and so on.

Attribute Number to Computer for Credibility

Sometimes, convenient numbers are used innocently by persons who do not understand numbers. The devious convenient number user will never explain how he arrived at the number except to say that he got it from an impeachable source, or from a notable publication, or from the media. More recently, a source frequently quoted is the computer (as though it has superior knowledge of any subject).

Blame the Computer

Computers hardly ever make mistakes. If you enter into a computer *x#?p* to mean John, the computer will respond *x#?p*. It repeats your error. When a computer errs, you can bet that it is an easily recognized breakdown. It is *not* a *subtle* error too difficult to detect. The greatest asset the computer has for a devious number user is that it accepts blame without complaint. In a word, the buck stops at the computer.

SUMMARY

We have seen in this chapter that numbers thrust at you are for the convincing power they have. Manipulation of such numbers is usually straightforward but most often the manipulation is illogical as in the use of per capita figures to allot land, or the numbers are virtually pulled out of the air as was the 1500-ad exposure per day. If a reliable-appearing source is frequently cited, you can bet that the numbers have been manipulated in some way. When no reliable sources are cited you can also bet that the numbers are contrived.

Remember one thing. Most convenient numbers sound rational. Therefore, you must be even more watchful. The more you question a number, the more likely you are to uncover the truth. An unscrupulous numbers user will back off quickly when faced with a forceful challenge. Try it.

What to Do

Not all numbers thrust at you are fake. However, you should have at least a method of detecting those that are fake.

Before passing on to your audience a number that you have little or no idea how it was derived, ask the provider to give you an explanation of how the number was acquired: the source, and how it was calculated. If you are satisfied with the explanation, use it. However, if it is a bogus number, the provider will not know the source or how the number was calculated. The more naive provider will merely say that it was computer generated. Sometimes organizations or persons that are known to have credibility are cited. You should contact that source because, like a statement passed on several times, the meaning changes in the process. Sometimes the previous provider cited may be your story. So be careful. You do not want to be a spreader of a bogus number virus.

7

Probable Probabilities: Don't Bet on Them

"Tell you what I am going to do! I have here three shells. I am going to put this pea under one of the shells. If you correctly tell me under which shell the pea is, I'll give you ten dollars. If you guess wrong, you give me ten dollars." Is this little game familiar to you?

PART OF OUR LIVES

The deal is that probabilities of things happening or not happening are as much a part of our lives as ice cream. We wish people good luck, bad luck, and sometimes no luck at all. Some people make a profit from probabilities; many are fooled by them at one time or another. Some businesses prosper by the sole use of probabilities; insurance companies, casinos, and lotteries are a few. In order for these companies to succeed, the odds must favor them in some way. Even if the shell game was honest, the odds of you winning are 1 in 3. Yet you win only even money.

Life Expectancy Data

When you take out a life insurance policy, the insurance company is betting on the probability that you will live long enough to pay all the premiums to cover the face value of the policy and then some. Conversely, you are betting that you will die before all the premiums are paid. Insurance companies have life expectancy data with which to calculate such probabilities and thus set the premium payments accordingly. Should you win the bet, you have the comfort of knowing that your survivors will have the money to bury you.

Calculating Probabilities: Sometimes Easy, Sometimes Difficult

Calculating the probability of something occurring may be simple at times and complex at other times. When playing cards, for example, the probability of drawing, say, the King of Spades from a full deck of freshly shuffled cards is 1 in 52. The probability of drawing any other card instead is 51 in 52. The odds of drawing the King of Spades are 1 to 51. The odds of drawing any other card are 51 to 1.

After a hand is dealt, there is no way of calculating the probability of drawing the King of Spades as the next card unless you can see all the cards that have been previously dealt. However, if 30 cards have been dealt, five cards to each of six players, the probability that the King of Spades is among the cards dealt is 30 in 52. The probability that the King of Spades is still in the deck is 22 in 52. The odds, then, are 30 to 22 that the King of Spades has been dealt.

If you have been dealt one of those hands and you were not dealt the King of Spades, the probability that the King of Spades has been dealt to the other five players is 25 in 47. The probability that it has not been dealt to the other players is 22 in 47. The odds that the King of Spades has been dealt are 25 to 22. Having seen your hand changed the odds and gave you more insight into the situation. This is what this chapter is about. The more you know about the situation, the more likely you are of making a smarter decision.

Game of Dice

In the game of dice, each die has six sides, numbered 1 to 6. It is not too difficult to calculate the probability that two dice, thrown simultaneously, any sum from 2 to 12 will land face up. There are 36 possible outcomes in such a procedure. Table 7.1 gives the probabilities for each possibility.

If the dice are not loaded — that is, weighted in some way — the probabilities are the same for each roll. In the game of craps the shooter (the person rolling the dice) loses, if on his first attempt, he rolls either 2 or 3 or 12. He wins if he rolls 7 or 11. He has one chance in 36 to roll 2; two chances to roll 3; and one chance to roll 12. Therefore, he has four chances in 36 to lose. He has six chances in 36 to roll 7, and two chances to roll 11, or eight chances in 36 to win on the first roll. The odds of winning on the first roll are 8 to 4. The probability of neither winning nor losing on the first roll — that is, rolling any number from 4 to 10 — is 24 in 36. The odds of rolling a number from 4 to 10 before 7 or 11 are 24 to 8, or 3 to 1.

Having rolled a number from 4 to 10, what are the odds

TABLE 7.1
Probabilities in the Game of Dice

2 > 1+1	1/36
3 > 1+2, 2+1	2/36
4 > 1+3, 3+1, 2+2	3/36
5 > 1+4, 4+1, 2+3, 3+2	4/36
6 > 1+5, 5+1, 2+4, 4+2, 3+3	5/36
7 > 1+6, 6+1, 2+5, 5+2, 3+4, 4+3	6/36
8 > 2+6, 6+2, 3+5, 5+3, 4+4	5/36
9 > 3+6, 6+3, 4+5, 5+4	4/36
10 > 4+6, 6+4, 5+5	3/36
11 > 5+6, 6+5	2/36
12 > 6+6	1/36

that 7 will be rolled before the other number? The odds of rolling 7 before 6 or 8 are 6 to 5. The odds of rolling 7 before 5 or 9 are 6 to 4, or 3 to 2. The odds of rolling 7 before 4 or 10 are 6 to 3, or 2 to 1.

Odds on Winning a Lottery

Many gambling probabilities can be calculated in advance. Some require exceptional mental skills even to approximate the odds. States often publish the probability of winning and the payoff of a lottery. For example, in a lottery of six numbers selected randomly out of 44, the probability of guessing all six numbers correctly is 1 in 7,059,052. The probability of correctly guessing five out of the six winning numbers is 1 in 30,961. Usually, the payoff is not nearly as much as the risk a player takes. How else could the state make a profit? Odds on slot machines, for example, cannot be calculated unless one can get information from the manufacturer or the casino on how many symbols are on each reel of a slot machine.

In our day-to-day living, we usually do not encounter probabilities that we can calculate. We see probabilities on the likelihood of precipitation, of getting a certain disease, of being struck by lightning, and of other similar occurrences. Have you ever wondered *how* these probabilities are calculated?

PRINCIPLE OF CALCULATING PROBABILITY

In simple terms, probabilities are calculated by dividing the number of times a certain event happens by the total number of times it is possible for that event to happen. In dice or cards or other forms of gambling, the conditions are explicit in the game. Whether you play poker in the living room, or in the kitchen, or in China, or standing on your head makes no difference to the probabilities inherent in the game. In other instances the rub comes, first, in knowing the accuracy of the number of occurrences and, second, in knowing the accuracy of the total number of possibilities. It is also important to know the area from which these counts are made. The likelihood of someone dying of a heart attack in Switzerland might be different from someone in the United States. We usually presume that when a certain probability is given, it applies universally, but that is not the case.

Conditional Probabilities

The likelihood of being struck by lightening in Tampa, Florida, is greater than in Rochester, New York. The answer is logical. Although the population of both cities is approximately the same, Tampa has many more lightning storms than Rochester.

If the U. S. Census Bureau reports that 31% of the total population is 45 years or older, we take it that the probability is 1 in 3 that the next person we see will be 45 years or older. It does not follow that every third person is in that age group. In some places they may be bunched. If you are in a high school, that probability is not likely to prevail.

General Probabilities Versus Specific Probabilities

The mass media say much about the probability of dying from certain causes. They say that heart disease is the biggest killer and that 1 in 3 will die of that disease. What is the likelihood that you will die of that disease? I'll tell you my likelihood. It is nearly 100%. Here's why. I am male, and men are more likely to contract heart disease than women, although women seem to be catching up. On top of that my father died of heart disease. My mother died of it also as did my oldest sister. My older sister has heart disease and so have I. It is very, very likely that the cause of my death will be heart disease. Of course, I could arrange to be shot by a

jealous husband. The likelihood would be much greater that
I would be shot by my wife.

THE ODDS ON RUSSIAN ROULETTE

Russian Roulette is played with a six-shooter, having
one chamber loaded while the other five chambers in the
cylinder are empty. If the cylinder is spun before each
squeeze of the trigger, the odds are 5:1 the gun will not
fire. Each spin of the cylinder and its subsequent
squeeze of the trigger become one independent event.
Each event has the same odds.

However, if the cylinder is not spun before each
event, the odds depend on the outcome of the previous
event. The odds on the first event are 5:1. The odds that
the gun will not fire decrease by one until the pistol
fires. For example, the odds before the first squeeze of
the trigger are 5:1. If the gun does not fire, the odds of
it not firing decrease to 4:1, then 3:1, and so on until
there is only one chamber left. Then, bang!

Anecdotal Probabilities

Sometimes we are exposed to anecdotal probabilities. A
person interviewing on a street corner, not aware of being
near an unemployment office, may come away with the
notion that the majority of people is unemployed.

Probabilities Based on Statistics

Statistics provide probabilities on numerous subjects. For
example, a national magazine reported that of 1,000 divorced
women, 35 to 39 years of age, 89.7 remarried. This translates
into the probability that if you are a woman, 35 to 39 years
old, you stand a 9% chance of remarrying. No mention is
made that perhaps, after having had a bad first marriage,

you do not choose to marry again. Or, that perhaps you got a divorce because you had another marital candidate standing by.

Statistics also show that persons driving alone have 30% fewer automobile accidents. To avoid the risk of an automobile accident, the next time your spouse wants to go shopping with you, drive there in different cars.

The Probability That It Will Rain

A probability we see and hear each day is the likelihood of precipitation, or the percent chance of rain. Ever wonder how this probability is calculated. It took a telephone call to Washington, D.C., before I could get an inkling of how this number is calculated. Mind you I said "inkling." It is still not too clear in my mind.

According to a spokesman at the United States Weather Service, the percentage is calculated by several computer models of atmospheric motion. Measurable data such as wind velocity and direction, temperature, air pressure and density at various levels are fed into these computers. The results determine when the air will rise or fall and the speed by which it does. The speed of the rise motion is translated into position on a scale ranging from 0 to 100%. The rub is that meteorologists *may* alter the computer findings if they choose.

Our own knowledge tells us that air rises slowly in the winter causing drizzles and slow rains. Air rises quickly in the summer causing showers and thunderstorms. Thus, it is better to wear running shoes more often in the summer to make those dashes for cover.

At what percentage should you carry an umbrella? Well, at a 50% chance of rain, it could go either way. In my opinion, when the chance it will rain is above 50%, carry an umbrella. When the chance of rain is less than 50%, don't. When the chance is 50% exactly, flip a coin. Chances are that you will be wrong as often as you will be right.

PROBABILITY SHIBBOLETHS

Before there were mechanisms for verifying the sex of an unborn child, there were probably as many methods of predicting the sex of an unborn child as there were pregnant women. Our pediatrician had a unique system. Each time my wife visited him during a pregnancy, he would predict the sex of the baby. He would predict a boy on one visit. On the next visit he would predict a girl. He continued alternating his prediction until the baby was born. Then, after the baby was born, he would say with much attention-getting fanfare, "I told you so."

What are the chances that when someone asked you to put out your hands that you would put them out palms up? A woman I knew used to ask pregnant women to put out their hands. She predicted that when the pregnant woman put out her hands palms up, the baby would be a girl; palms down, a boy. I didn't put too much stock in this method until I learned that she was right most of the time.

PROBABILITY SCAMS

Some connivers made money on predicting the sex of unborn children. Because the total population has almost an equal number of males or females born, we can say that the odds are 50/50. To make money using this probability, a self-styled guru would charge $10 to predict the sex of an unborn child. Half of the time he predicted girls, the other half boys. If the prediction turned out to be incorrect, he gladly refunded $10. He kept the $10 from those he predicted correctly. On the average he made $5 on every prediction he made, right or wrong. Too bad technology ruined his act.

The amount of creativity going into ways of relieving people of their money has no limits. You may receive, free, several correct predictions on the movement of the stock market. Then, just as you gain confidence in the predictor, he may ask you to pay for his next prediction. Don't do it. The scam is that opposite predictions are sent to others. He continues to send predictions only to those who have received all correct predictions. Although his list gets smaller each time he drops those who were sent an incorrect prediction, if his initial list is sufficiently large, he still makes a great deal of money.

Mention probabilities to most people and you will see a gleam in their eyes. Everyone thinks he can beat the odds. To those I say good luck. To everyone else, particularly reporters who pass out these numbers to others, I say, learn as much as you can beforehand. You will find that the probabilities you thought were right were not right. The more you know about a situation, the more likely you are of making the correct decision. Remember there are no free lunches, but there are plenty of people out there who are figuring out ways to eat *your* lunch.

SUMMARY

Probabilities can be useful to put across desired emotional environment. Some probabilities are easy to calculate, others are difficult, if not impossible, to calculate. The idea is that probabilities are merely averages of the likelihood of something happening or not happening without regard for any influential effects. For example, Norman Cousins, past editor of the *Saturday Review,* laughed his way to beat the odds against recovering from painful collagen illness by viewing, reading, and doing those things that would make him laugh.

What to Do

As a journalist, it is incumbent upon you to divulge at least the conditions under which the probabilities are calculated. For example, if you are reporting the likelihood of someone surviving a certain type of surgery, it would be important to also report the number of operations that this likelihood is based on, the area from which that number was drawn (i.e., the city, state, nation, etc.), and during what period of time.

When reporting the likelihood of precipitation, it would be a good idea to run a box giving a brief explanation of how the percent probability was calculated and a description of the area covered. It could be a standard box run every several weeks. You may find that your audience will be more forgiving when the forecast is incorrect.

The Law of Large Numbers:
You Lose

When I was a boy I used to hear men, while listening to baseball games on the radio, refer to a batter's likelihood of getting a hit. They would say he was bound to get a hit now because he had not had a hit in several previous times at bat. They referred this logic to the law of averages. It wasn't until I studied statistics in later years that I learned they were referring to the Law of Large Numbers.

DEFINITION

According to the Law of Large Numbers, the more we repeat an action, the closer we come to the theoretical or true probability of its occurrence. The probabilities in gambling are good examples. Consider flipping a coin. We know that the true probability of a coin landing heads up or tails up is 50%. Put another way, before every flip of a coin the odds are 1/1, or 50/50 as we are used to referring to them.

As you can imagine, it is impossible to achieve the true odds, 50/50, if we flip the coin only once. On the first flip the result is either 100/0, or 0/100. As Chart 8.1 indicates, as we flip the coin many more times, we shall come closer to achieving the true ratio. According to the Law of Large Numbers, we can be confident that if we flip a coin 10 times, we can expect to achieve a ratio no wider than 80/20, or 20/80. If we flip a coin 100 times, we can expect to achieve a ratio of heads to tails or vice-versa no wider than 60/40. The result of flipping a coin 10,000 times will reduce the spread from the true odds to 2 percentage points, 51/49.

Gambling Casinos

There is no way that gambling casinos can survive without the Law of Large Numbers. Casinos depend on the billions of times their games and devices are played. That is why there are gambling devices in every area of the casino and the casinos remain open day and night.

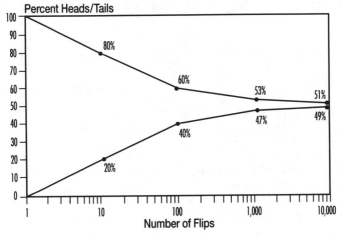

CHART 8.1.

Casinos Operate on Small Advantage. The casinos make money because they have a slight edge over the true odds. When large numbers of plays are made, a slight advantage in the odds is sufficient to make a substantial income.

Roulette

To illustrate, consider roulette as played in American casinos. The board and the wheel contain 38 numbers from 1 to 36, plus 0 and 00. One-half, 18, of the 36 numbers are colored red; the other 18 are colored black. One-half, 18, of the 36 numbers are odd; the other 18 are even. Zero (0) and double zero (00) are neither black or red, nor odd or even.

Table 8.1 gives you an idea of the advantage a casino has between the true odds against the player and the payoff in roulette. The house advantage may be more, or less, for other games and gambling devices. However, the advantage always belongs to the house.

Notice that the casino has a small advantage on every bet situation. Casinos must have at least a small advantage on every game they play or they could not stay in business. The

TABLE 8.1
Payoff Ratios versus True Odds American Roulette

The Bet on:	Payoff	True Odds	House Advantage
Any Individual Number (1–36, 0, 00)	35:1	37:1	5%
Two Adjacent Numbers	17:1	18:1	6%
Row – 3 Numbers	11:1	11.67:1	6%
A Square – 4 Numbers	8:1	8.5:1	6%
Two Consecutive Rows – 6 Numbers	5:1	5.33:1	6%
One Column – 12 Numbers	2:1	2.17:1	8%
Numbers 1–12, or 13–24, or 25–36	2:1	2.17:1	8%
Red or Black, Odds or Event, Low (any number 1–18) High (any number 19–36)	1:1	1.11:1	10%

overall marketing strategy of every casino is to stimulate very large numbers of bets daily. It is the only way they can successfully utilize the effects of the Law of Large Numbers.

Habitual Player Destined to Lose

Conversely, the Law of Large Numbers works against the individual casino player if he habitually plays. Look at it this way. If you try to squeeze through the funnel as depicted in Chart 8.1, the more times you play, the narrower the opening becomes. When you squeeze through the end, you will be wrung out and the only friends you will have will be the pawnbrokers.

Most people never attempt to go that far. It is fun to gamble when the stakes are affordable. Sometimes we might even walk away with a pocket full of money. Sometimes.

State Lotteries

State lotteries have been around for centuries as a way of financing government. They have become more popular in America in recent years for the same reason. I don't know of any state lottery that has not been successful. They should be. The advantage state lotteries have in payoffs versus true odds makes casinos look like sugar daddies.

State Lotteries Operate on Big Advantage

While casinos operate on a small advantage, state lotteries operate on a very big advantage. For example, one state pays 499/1 on Pick 3 numbers from 0 to 9 in correct order. The true odds against the player are 999/1 – 100% advantage for the state. The same state, on pick 6 numbers from 1 to 44, pays off 1,000,000/1. The true odds against the player are 7,059,051/1, or an advantage for the state of 600%. I suppose the state should have a big advantage in the odds. How else could it raise money quickly?

Winner's Payoff in Annual Installments

On top of that, when a player wins the million dollars, the payoff is in 20 equal installments annually. It takes 19 years for the winner to collect all the winnings. The first installment is paid immediately. No interest is paid on the balance the state holds.

Often the winner is publicly photographed holding a giant-size check for the full amount of the jackpot. The winner does not receive the amount he is promised in the publicity. The state pays only the first installment. The state needs to have on-hand only the amount of the first installment. It would seem fitting to buy the lottery ticket in 20 installments.

Another state recently announced a "new improved super lotto," in which players select two sets of 6 numbers from 1 to 50. The chance of winning with one set or the other set of 6 numbers is 1 in 7,945,350. The jackpot was raised to $3 million, but the payments were spread over 26 annual installments. Soon you will need to buy a lottery ticket when you are 4 years old if you expect to live long enough to receive all the installments.

Besides waiting for the payoff, which limits the winner's ability to make big purchases, the winner loses all the interest the money would earn over 19 years of installments. In addition, the purchasing power of the remainder will decrease each year as prices continue to rise.

What the State Could Do with the Money
It Owes the Winner

This is what might happen to the money owed to a $1 million winner (Table 8.2). By investing the balance after the first installment at 7% simple annual interest rate, the state will have accrued over $1.5 million while paying the winner each installment on time. Pretty neat, eh?

So, the state pays $1,000,000 and takes in $1,566,755 with

TABLE 8.2
Investment on $950,000* at 7% Annual Interest

Year	*Balance After $50,000 Installment	Year End 1st Col.x1.07	Installment Amount	Installment Number
1	$ 950,000	$1,016,500	− $50,000	2
2	966,500	1,034,155	− 50,000	3
3	984,155	1,053,046	− 50,000	4
4	1,003,046	1,073,259	− 50,000	5
5	1,023,259	1,094,888	− 50,000	6
6	1,044,888	1,118,030	− 50,000	7
7	1,068,030	1,142,792	− 50,000	8
8	1,092,792	1,169,287	− 50,000	9
9	1,119,287	1,197,637	− 50,000	10
10	1,147,637	1,227,972	− 50,000	11
11	1,177,972	1,260,430	− 50,000	12
12	1,210,430	1,295,160	− 50,000	13
13	1,245,160	1,332,322	− 50,000	14
14	1,282,322	1,372,084	− 50,000	15
15	1,322,084	1,414,630	− 50,000	16
16	1,364,630	1,460,154	− 50,000	17
17	1,410,154	1,508,865	− 50,000	18
18	1,458,865	1,560,986	− 50,000	19
19	1,510,986	1,616,755	− 50,000	20
20	1,566,755			

the winner's money. After the fourth installment, the winner is not only paying himself but he is earning a superb profit for the state. Moreover, it is likely that an initial investment of $950,000 will attract more than 7% interest, creating an even more profitable situation for the state.

Not Enough Money for Lump Sum Payoffs

Another disturbing element: It has been said that states do not have the money to pay off jackpots in a lump sum. Probably the state would buy an annuity that would meet the annual payments. If all goes well over the 19-year period, the winner will receive all the money. If the institution providing the annuity goes bankrupt during the payment period, the winner may lose part or all of the remaining balance.

WHAT THE MONEY IN THE WINNER'S POCKET CAN DO

Some persons reason that federal taxes on a lump sum payment of $1,000,000 would be astronomical. However, the maximum federal income tax on $1,000,000 is 31%, or $310,000. If tax liabilities and the winner's spending spree consumed half of the jackpot, the remaining $500,000 will grow to over $1.8 million during the 19-year span if invested at 7% interest rate, compounded annually. Of course, the winner has many other investment options that are likely to produce more revenue.

Effect of Inflation over 19 Years

If this isn't enough, consider what happens to the purchasing power of the jackpot over 19 annual installments. Allowing for a modest 4% annual inflation rate, $50,000 the winner receives as the last payment will have the purchasing power of $23,021.

If you do not expect to live for 20 more years, you may not want to consider playing the lottery. A man in his middle 70s recently won $1,000,000 in a state lottery. After 20% federal tax withholding and 4% tax withholding by the state, he received a first payment of $38,000. It is possible that he will live to collect every installment, but that is another bet.

SUMMARY

Simply stated, the Law of Large Numbers accommodates the idea that the more we repeat an event, the closer that event becomes to its predictable level. Journalists seldom need to report on it except when it affects the public, as in state lotteries.

This chapter was not intended to convince journalists to become super critics of casinos or state lotteries. It *is* intended to illustrate how the Law of Large Numbers works in a practical environment. Remember. When the odds favor the players, the Law of Large Numbers will be their friend. When the odds favor the house, advise the players to quit when the fun goes out of the game, unless they enjoy doing business with pawn brokers.

Correlation: Obscure Causality

Because two sets of numbers are observed to correlate, or increase or decrease simultaneously, it does not follow that one set caused the other to happen. Most often that kind of relationship is mere coincidence. Successful propagandists, however, make frequent use of correlation and causality, and its coincidental occurrence.

USEFUL STATISTICAL TOOL

Correlation analysis is a useful statistical tool. Statisticians calculate correlation coefficients to determine whether two sets of numbers vary harmoniously or not. The numbers 4, 3, 5, 1, 2 and 2, 4, 10, 8, 6 are in discord. They have no similar varying pattern and therefore have no correlation, or have a correlation coefficient of zero.

Correlation Coefficient

The numbers 1, 2, 3, 4, 5 and 2, 4, 6, 8, 10 vary in perfect positive harmony. Thus, they have a correlation coefficient of +1. It can be said that when one number goes up in one set, we can expect that its corresponding number in the other set will go up in the same proportion.

The numbers 1, 2, 3, 4, 5 and 10, 8, 6, 4, 2 vary in perfect negative harmony having a correlation coefficient of -1. Under this condition, we can expect that when one number goes up in one set, its partner in the other set will go down similarly.

It hardly ever happens that sets of numbers vary in perfect *positive* harmony. Those coefficients appear somewhere between 0 and 1 which makes interpretation of the relationship more difficult. Even if the numbers always appeared in perfect harmony, proving that one caused the other is difficult indeed. Often the relationship is coincidental.

Statisticians grapple with causality almost daily and even the most objective statisticians are sometimes fooled. But, a person bent on illustrating his point of view can use correlation, often mere coincidence, to persuasively prove causation.

Spurious Causality

If I told you that the United States was losing the war with Japan until I joined the Marines, then started to win, would you believe that I was the cause of the turnaround? Hardly. The following illustration is more convincing, however.

A news item appearing in a daily newspaper reported that a spokesman for the American Cancer Society "links the decline in lung cancer death rates with a significant decline in cigarette consumption." He credits not smoking cigarettes as the cause for the decline of lung cancer rates. More efficient emission controls on automobiles, cleaner air in homes and offices resulting from improved air filtration, reduction of pollutants in the atmosphere, and more successful treatment of cancer receive no credit at all.

The Wrong Variable

I used to work for a newspaper in Florida as a researcher and statistician. Our sales records indicated that there was a high negative correlation between sales volume and educational attainment of the sales staff. Salespersons with less formal education produced more advertising sales volume, whereas salespersons with more education produced less sales volume. According to these findings, a person with more than an eighth grade education need not apply for a position as a salesperson in our advertising department.

The correlation here isn't distorted. In this case, educational attainment is the wrong criterion for successful salesmanship. Seniority would have been a better predictor than education. Here's why. Salespersons with less education are older. They joined the company when educational attainment was not as important as it is today. They have been with the company longer than the better educated salespersons. Consequently, they have the larger accounts that buy more advertising.

Shoe Size and Mathematical Ability

William F. Buckley, Jr., in the *Richmond News Leader,* January 9, 1990, quoted from an essay by Professor Thomas Sowell, who wrote: "The potential for misleading explanations can be illustrated with a simple example. Shoe size undoubtedly correlates with test scores on advanced mathematical examinations, in the sense that people with size 3 shoes probably cannot, on the average, answer as many questions correctly as people with size 12 shoes—the former being much more likely to be younger children and the latter more likely to be older children or adults. Thus shoe size 'explains' part of the math score difference—in the special sense in which statisticians use the word. But nobody can expect to do better on a math test by wearing larger shoes on the day it is taken. In the real sense of the word, shoe size explains nothing."

More Pages of Rules, Fewer Members

A colleague recently presented me with another illustration of spurious causality. He pointed out that between 1985 and

1987, as the number of pages of the rule book of the United States Boomerang Association increased, its membership decreased accordingly. It would suggest, then, that by printing the rules on fewer pages, the declining membership would turn around. The reason for the decline was due to the nature of the boomerang and not the number of pages in the rule book. Boomerangs create sudden intense interest among first-time observers until they discover the secret that makes the boomerangs return. Then the interest declines with the same quick intensity.

Income Versus Auto Ownership

The correlation between owning expensive automobiles and personal income is another illustration of the folly of causation when only a small amount of information is known. Is it because a person has more money that he buys expensive cars or because he buys expensive cars that he makes more money? Some people buy expensive cars just to make you believe they make a lot of money.

Back-Flipping Insect

A scientist trained an insect to do a backflip on the command, "Jump." He noted that, on issuing the command, the insect performed a backflip with ease. He removed one leg from the insect, set the insect down on the table and issued the command. He noted that upon removing one leg, the insect performed the backflip with little difficulty.

He removed another leg from the insect, issued the command, and noted that with the insect's two remaining legs, it successfully performed the backflip but with greater difficulty. The scientist removed the insect's third leg and called out the command. He noted that with one remaining leg, the insect was able to perform the backflip but it took several tries and much more effort.

He removed the insect's last leg. He called out the com-

mand and nothing happened. He called out several times.
Jump! Jump! Jump! The insect did not move. Reluctantly,
he noted that upon removing the last leg, the insect turned
deaf.

THREE CONDITIONS FOR CAUSALITY

Generally, there are three conditions that must be present
before one may say, with some assurance, that something
caused another thing to happen (Babbie, 1979)[1]:

1. The causal variable must occur before, in time, the
   effect variable occurs.
2. There should be an observed reality between the perceived cause and effect variables. For example, if
   there are no instances of injury, how can one say that
   throwing boomerangs causes bodily injury?
3. The relationship is found to be the result of some
   other cause having an effect on the initial variables.
   To illustrate, there may be a high correlation between
   existence of churches and criminal acts. One may
   erroneously conclude that churches cause crime. The
   reality is that where there are many churches, there are
   many people, and where there is more crime, there are
   many people. The existence of people is the third
   variable affecting the building of churches and the
   encouragement of crime.

SUMMARY

This chapter takes into account errors made in recognizing
causal relationships and how some people use coincidental
occurrences to imply causality. Before accepting a causal

---

[1]BABBIE, E. R. (1979). *The Practice of Social Research* (2nd ed.).
Belmont, CA: Wadsworth Publishing Company, Inc.

relationship, make certain that, in your opinion, it meets the three conditions set forth in the box.

Be skeptical of those who take credit for, or lay blame on, an event because it happened in concert with another, particularly when you sense a strong motive. You can bet that rain will make your grass grow. But you can also bet that too much rain will kill your grass.

Remember. Superstitions are made from false causes.

Sampling: A Few Represent Many

Without oversimplifying, we can say that the phenomenon of sampling has been intuitive since the beginning of time, albeit in a not-so-scientific way. Your mother knows intuitively how to taste the flavor of a pot of soup. She doesn't drink the whole pot to make certain that it all tastes good. Instead, she stirs the soup, takes out a tablespoon, and tastes it. If it tastes all right, she is satisfied that the whole pot of soup has the same taste.

Your doctor is satisfied taking just a small vial of blood from you to test the balance of its chemistry. Imagine the consequences if he didn't believe in sampling. Similarly, a vintner needs to taste only a few bunches of grapes at the appropriate time to get an idea of the flavor of the forthcoming wine.

BEYOND HAPHAZARD METHODS

The phenomenon of sampling, in which few represent many, goes beyond simple unscientific methods such as tasting soup. Because data is often too difficult to obtain from infinitely large numbers of units, such as people, data is obtained from a small sample or cross-section, representing the whole, or the universe, as statisticians call it.

Universality of Sampling

Imagine how difficult it would be to interview every person in the labor force in the United States to determine the unemployment rate. Instead the United States Government scientifically samples about 60,000 households and interviews members of the labor force in these households. From this cross-section, the government predicts what percent of the entire labor force is unemployed and looking for work.

Airlines' Use of Sampling

When you buy an airline ticket, the first airline you go to tickets you through your entire trip, even if you have to use other airlines to get there and back. The ticket-initiating airline collects the entire fare. Accordingly, if other airlines are involved, the ticket-initiating airline must pay other airlines involved their portion of the total fare. To do this, the airline would have to analyze thousands of tickets it sold every month and make the appropriate payments to other airlines. Instead, the initiating airline has a bilateral agreement with every other airline on the sample size. The average sample size is 10%, although when many tickets are involved, the sample may be as small as one-half of 1%. The ticket-initiating airline pays other airlines a projected amount, based on the sample.

Every Unit Must Have Equal Chance
of Being Selected

Airlines have confidence in the system because the samples are drawn by scientifically designed random methods. The principle of representative or cross-section sampling is straightforward and simple. Each unit (ticket) in the *universe* (all the tickets of the initiating airline for the month) must have an equal chance of being selected. It is not necessary to know the chance of being selected. One only needs to know that each unit has an equal chance. For example, samples drawn from telephone numbers present no opportunity for any household without a telephone to be selected.

Scientific Sampling

Designing a scientifically random sample is usually more difficult than one might imagine. If 1,000 airline tickets were to be drawn from 10,000 tickets, one would select a starting point, from 1 to 9, at random then select every tenth ticket. If the number 6 was drawn from numbers 1 to 9, then the first selection would be the 6th ticket, then the 16th, 26th, 36th, and so on.

If every unit must have an equal chance of being selected for a sample to be representative, it does not figure that a poll conducted over the airwaves or as an insert in a publication will meet this criterion. In polls of this type, a person chooses himself to be included in the sample. Findings of this type represent only those who chose to respond, usually persons who feel strongly about the subject under study. One can alter the results by responding many times to the same poll.

Almost Anything Can Be Sampled

Adults, children, nurses, lawyers, fire hydrants, automobiles, street corners all can be sampled. Samples may be drawn of just about anything. Each requires its own sampling design. To select a sample of pediatricians in the United States, for example, one needs only to acquire the list from the American Medical Association. Scientifically selecting a representative sample of noninstitutionalized persons 35 to 54 years of age requires more ingenuity and effort.

Sampling People

Sampling airline tickets is one thing. Sampling people is another. Sometimes people cannot be reached when the survey is conducted and some refuse to answer. Unless 100% of those sampled is contacted and responds, the phenomenon of sampling does not work. If only 50% of the sample of pediatricians answered the questionnaire, the results would be doubtful at best.

Completion Rate

Unfortunately the American public has been deluged by a growing number of telephone solicitations, many of which pretend to be conducting surveys. As a consequence, the public is reluctant to respond to survey questions. Statisticians have had to compromise. If a survey successfully achieves a minimum of 70% completion, statisticians are now likely to accept findings from surveys pertaining to opinions or attitudes.

Sampling Tolerance

Once the sample has been selected so that every unit in the universe to be studied has an equal chance of being selected and a completion rate of 70% or more has been achieved, precision of the findings can be calculated. This is often reported as the *sampling tolerance* or *sampling error*. It is always reported as a percentage point, never as a percent, and is usually given as a percentage point plus or minus. What it means is that a finding such as 40% that has a 5 percentage point, plus or minus, tolerance is likely to fall between 35% and 45% if all the units were studied. In other words, if we repeated the study a year later and obtained a result of 43%, we would have to conclude that no change occurred. To reflect a change, the percentage would have to be below 35% and above 45%.

Factors Affecting Sampling Tolerance

Generally, two factors affect the amount of the sampling tolerance: sample size and the degree of unanimity of the response or observation. The closer the result is to 50%, the larger the sampling tolerance given the same sample size. A larger sample will have a smaller sampling tolerance, given the same degree of unanimity.

Bear in mind that this works only when the sample has been drawn in a way that provides an equal chance for every unit in the study universe to be selected. Also bear in mind that a sampling tolerance calculated for the total sample does not apply to any segment of the sample. Sampling tolerance for a segment of the sample must be calculated from the size of the segment. If a sampling tolerance is given for a sample of men and women, then data is reported for women only; the sampling tolerance must be calculated for the number of women in the sample.

Table 10.1 illustrates sampling tolerances, in percentage points, for most popular sample sizes.

TABLE 10.1
Sampling Tolerance (Percentage Points, Plus or Minus)

Sample Size	Response				
	10%/90%	20%/80%	30%/70%	40%/60%	50%/50%
100	5.9	7.8	9.0	9.6	9.8
300	3.4	4.5	5.2	5.5	5.7
500	2.6	3.5	4.0	4.3	4.4
1,000	1.9	2.5	2.8	3.0	3.1
1,500	1.5	2.0	2.3	2.5	2.5
2,000	1.3	1.8	2.0	2.1	2.2
3,000	1.1	1.4	1.6	1.8	1.8

HOW TO READ TABLE 10.1

If 10% of a sample of 300 (second row) gave a certain response, say, "yes," reading across to the column headed "10% or 90%," we see 3.4 percentage points, plus or minus. This means that if a census were taken of the universe represented by a sample of 300, we should expect a "yes" response would fall between 10 plus or minus 3.4 percentage points, or between 6.6% and 13.4%.

It follows that if 10% responded "yes," then 90% did not respond "yes." Therefore, the same tolerance applies to the percent who did not give a "yes" response, 90 − 3.4 and 90 + 3.4, or between 86.6% and 93.4%.

Notice as you read down the sample-size column that, as the sample size becomes larger, the precision improves—that is, the percentage-point tolerance becomes smaller. Notice, too, that as you read across nearing 50%/50%, you are moving away from unanimity and thus the sampling tolerance becomes larger. This tells us that you don't need a very large sample to get reliable response if you ask people to choose between the devil and God. But you will need a large sample if you ask people to choose between green or blue.

LIKE MEASURING THE LENGTH OF A WALL

Sampling is very much like measuring the length of a wall. You first measure it with a tape measure calibrated in one-foot increments. It measures somewhere between 12 and 13 feet. Next, you measure it with a tape measure calibrated in half-foot increments. You notice that it measures between 25 and 26 "half" feet. You guess that it is about 25½ half feet. You then measure the same wall with a tape measure calibrated in one-inch increments. Your result turns out to be between 151 and 152 inches. You estimate 151½ inches. As you added more calibrations to your measuring instrument, your result became more precise and it would not have mattered if your wall was ten times as long. The level of the tolerance has to do with the size of the increment. The more calibrations you use, the more precise your result. Imagine that the number of calibrations represent the sample size. The larger the sample, the more precise your results become.

Same-Size Sample Can Represent Thousands or Millions

An important aspect of sampling is that a sample of 1,000 can represent 10,000, or 100,000, or 1,000,000, or 250,000,000 with the same degree of precision. Similarly, a person cooking a pot of soup samples the same amount for a large pot as for a small pot. A doctor does not withdraw more blood from a large person than he does from a small person. The sample representing 25,000 however must be drawn from the universe of 25,000, whereas the sample drawn to represent 250,000,000 must be drawn from that universe.

People and Their Opinions

The samples to which we are most exposed are those involving people and their opinions. There are many problems in sampling people, but three stand out: How does one find the people and reach them; how does one get their cooperation; and how does one pose the questions to achieve a clear understanding?

Misuse of Telephone Samples

Many polls simply use the telephone to reach whomever answers the telephone, unless it is a child or someone unsuitable for an interview conducted in English. If that person cooperates, the interview is logged as completed. If no one answers the telephone or the person who answers refuses to be interviewed, the interviewer dials other numbers until she or he gets the required number of interviews. Obviously, this method of sampling is not suitable for projecting to total people or total households no matter how many people answered the questions. There are those, too, who cannot be reached by telephone.

Misuse of Mail and Face-to-Face Samples

If the mail is used, results are often released from whatever percentage of the sample responded. Often, when personal, face-to-face interviews are used, refusals and not-at-homes are discounted. Under these circumstances, neither technique, regardless of the number responding, provides a suitable cross-section unless there is a 70% or more completion of the original sample.

Self-Selection Response Never Provides Reliable Representation

Obviously those surveys that give a viewer, listener, or a reader the option of responding by dialing a telephone to respond, or by completing a form and mailing it back, represent only the views of those *choosing* to respond. Samples using respondent self-selection seldom work. They cannot reliably represent the universe under study. Usually, the people queried who have strong feelings for or against the issue will respond. There are organizations, however, that compound the error. They poll via the 900 telephone exchange. Not only must people volunteer to respond, but must also pay a fee to do so. And, it is not uncommon among these organizations to report the findings as representative of "the people" or "Americans." Perhaps they should say "the gullible people" or "naive Americans."

How Slipshod Sampling Is Sometimes Disguised

Most professional research companies avoid dong slipshod sampling and they will not take on an assignment having such a stipulation. But, there are many amateurs doing public opinion polls who are not as scrupulous. You can recognize them easily. They give no details of the sample selection, completion ratios, or how the questions were phrased; they will emphasize the sampling tolerance to create an aura of credibility. In addition, you will find them using the word "scientific" often. Sometimes, they will tell you that the findings have been weighted to bring the sample into demographic balance. If the sample was drawn correctly in the first place and a decent completion ratio was achieved, the data would not have to be weighted. Besides which, how would they know the correct demographic balance.

Weighting is a post hoc procedure in survey research. After all the interviewing is completed, if it is discovered there are too few of a particular demographic group in the number of persons responding, the researcher gives added weight to those who responded from that particular group. If the researcher feels there should have been twice as many males responding to the survey, he multiplies the answer to each question given by a male by two. The implication is that the researcher knows how many should be in that group as well as every other group—how many men, how many women, how many whites, how many blacks, how many rich, how many poor, and so on. Then, too, adjusting for one group may throw off other groups in the sample. Some researchers use weighting techniques to avoid doing a more thorough, more expensive, interview follow-up. The computer has been a big help because it makes it easy to weight data. It used to be a long and tedious arithmetical process.

Extending the weighting idea all the way, a lazy researcher can interview a dozen well-chosen people, and by weighting, make the results look respectable. If you think this is absurd, think about this: Years ago there was a congressional investigation into a television rating service that had only one household representing all of the television households in the mountain states region of the United States. Some responsible weighting can be useful. However, how does one recognize responsible from irresponsible weighting without having the facts? The most media stories say about weighting is that "the sample was weighted to bring it into balance."

Implying Significance When There Is None

Recently, a newspaper story made much to do about an increase in the unemployment rate in the United States, from 5.2% in one month to 5.4% in the next month. The headline across two-thirds of the page read: "Jobless rate highest in 15 months." Television and radio stations picked up the story with the same level of hysteria. Announcement of the .2 percentage-point sampling tolerance from the issuing government agency usually goes unnoticed. Based on these numbers one would have to conclude that the sampling tolerance cast serious doubt on the interpretation made by the media.

Implying the Wrong Unit of Analysis

"The more a person knows about a lottery game, the more likely he is to buy a ticket," say two Virginia Commonwealth University professors who recently completed a year-long study of lottery players. Reading this newspaper story we would expect that "person" is any person, young or old, male or female, rich or poor. Unfortunately, the reader did not learn until several paragraphs later that the poll was conducted among students of that university—a sample representing only the student body, not the population as a whole.

Projecting Beyond the Scope of Survey

Try to figure out this one. "CATHOLIC DISSENT—A poll by the St. Paul, Minnesota, *Pioneer Press Dispatch* and

broadcast station WCCO found that strong majorities of
Roman Catholics—upwards of 60%—disagree with the
church's position prohibiting contraception, the marriage of
priests, and the ordination of women." No mention is made
of where the survey was conducted: St. Paul? Minnesota?
The United States? The story makes no mention of who was
interviewed, when the interviews took place, and the sample
size. Yet the term *Catholic Dissent* implies universal dissent
among all Catholics, everywhere. How much attention
should we give to this story? Zero attention.

Not Even a Majority Bothered to Respond

Results of another survey conducted by a Midwest daily
newspaper reported on attitudes of voters toward abortion
and legalized gambling. Fortunately for the reader, the story
did give the methodology; the survey cited a sampling
tolerance of plus or minus 2.2 percentage points, giving the
impression of a high degree of precision. However, the
newspaper said they adjusted the results to conform to the
universe under study. And, to their credit, they gave the
clincher as the last line of the story: "The response rate in the
poll was 23 percent." They shouldn't have bothered reporting
the results.

Beauty Is in the Eye of the Beholder

In another instance reported by the press, a financial house
mailed 1.1 million customer-service questionnaires. Only 278
completed and returned the questionnaire, achieving a response rate of .025%. With unbounded optimism, a company spokesman said, "That's an indication of customer
satisfaction." It would seem to me that it is customer apathy.
As it turned out, of the 278 who responded, 102, or 37%,
were pleased with the company's service. The chairman of the
company, who must be more optimistic than his spokesman,
considered the finding significant "that we are meeting many

clients' needs adequately." If 102 out of 1.1 million is "many," one has to wonder who taught him arithmetic.

It is in instances such as this that make us wonder if some who interpret survey findings are like the six blind men of Industan in the popular Indian legend. Each blind man felt a different part of the elephant and each described the elephant only according to the part he felt. The blind man who chanced to feel the knee of the elephant likened the elephant to a tree. The blind man who felt the tusk likened the elephant to a spear, and so on. Each man described the elephant only from his own perspective.

Self-Selected Judges

Several major newspapers in the United States gauge the popularity of comic strips, and keep or drop them, according to persons responding to a full-page ballot published in the newspaper. The idea is that the reader checks off his preferences and mails back the questionnaire at his expense. Pity that those who do not respond will have to settle for the comic strips selected by a few who responded who do not represent the total readership.

Once a questionnaire goes out to the public, the newspaper has no control over who answers. Think of this scenario: A person who thinks his favorite comic strip will be cancelled as a result of the survey, collects a bunch of newspapers and votes several times or gets friends to vote for his or her favorite comic strip. How is the newspaper to know?

Self-Selected Voters

You may recall that the same type of survey by the *Literary Digest* would have put Alf Landon in the White House. As it happened, in 1936, the *Literary Digest* mailed 10 million postcard ballots. A total of 2.4 million people responded. From that count, the *Literary Digest* predicted a Landon win over Roosevelt, 57% to 43%. Roosevelt won the election, 62.5% to 37.5%. Unfortunately, findings of poorly conducted polls can be disputed only by correctly conducting several similar polls, all of which would have to indicate the same differing results from the poorly conducted poll. It is much easier merely to ignore the results of a poorly conducted poll.

Very Few Respondents, Many Opinions

Another cunning method is the *focus group interview*. This technique brings ten or twelve persons into a room to discuss a certain issue. The group usually is led by a moderator who is supposed to keep the group focused on the subject. The purpose for this type of research is to have several knowledgeable people discuss and provide guidance to a researcher, who needs to learn the kinds of questions to ask about the subject in a formal survey. We might say that this is "research before research."

This method is simple and inexpensive to implement; therefore, many have passed off findings from focus groups as the research itself. Interpretations are presented as though the findings came from a bona fide cross-section survey. Findings from such groups represent the opinions of only those 10 or 12 persons participating in the focus group session.

Persons on the Street Represent
Only Themselves

Mass media, notably television, seem compelled to conduct person-on-the-street interviews. They often attribute the opinions of those few people to the entire population of an area. The implication is that, because we all appear on the street at one time or another, 3 or 4 people on the street represent everyone in the area. I have seen instances when a few people on the street have represented a city, a state, and even The United States. The words used to imply representation are: "Virginians say," or "And that's how New Yorkers think," or "That's how Americans feel about it."

Some person-on-the-street interviews are reported as scientific. Instead of reporting interviews on one street, some reporters interview on several streets. One medium in particular interviewed 12 persons on 12 difference streets. This medium attributed these opinions to the city's total adult population. This brings us to the notion of exit polls and random intercept polls which are extensions of the person-on-the-street poll. *Exit polls* interview voters as they leave their voting places. *Random intercept polls* interview people at some gathering place such as outside large stores or outside shopping centers. The idea, in both instances, is to stop people as they are passing by the interviewer. Although scientific samples of locations can be drawn, random selection of persons to be interviewed within the location is virtually impossible. At the time an interviewer is interviewing one person, she has no control over the numbers passing by that she misses. Given a choice of two passersby, the interviewer is likely to select a kind-looking person over a mean-looking person, or a person leisurely walking by over someone scurrying along. The poll is likely to get results *only* from sweet people who have the time to be interviewed.

SUMMARY

This chapter covered the points reporters need to know about survey sampling:

1. that the use of sampling is inherent in our lives;
2. that for a sample to be projectable to the universe, it must be selected so that every unit of analysis in the universe has an equal opportunity of being selected;
3. that the sample size as well as the unanimity of response affects the size of the sampling tolerance;
4. that respondents must be preselected at random and cannot have the opportunity to select themselves;

5. that a few respondents across a table or on the street represent only themselves; and

6. that a completion rate should be as close to 100% as possible (an acceptable level has been set at 70%).

Warning Signals

What to look out for when reading, viewing, or listening to results of polls:

1. No explanation is given of how the poll was conducted or who conducted it.

2. Sampling tolerance is given for the entire sample but findings are reported on subsamples such as men or women.

3. Minute differences are exaggerated or large differences are minimized.

4. No completion ratio is given.

5. There is a doubt that the question can be answered at all or by the communication method used—that is, the respondent knows nothing about the subject studied; the respondent cannot judge an illustration over the telephone or a sound by mail.

6. Those interviewed are asked to answer questions on the behavior of others—for instance, mother is asked to answer on out-of-home behavior of her teen-age children.

7. Findings are reported on a unit other than the sample unit—for instance, interviewing college students only and reporting the findings as total adults.

8. Results have been adjusted to "compensate for demographic differences between the sample and the actual demographic distribution." Ask yourself how the surveyors know the true demographic distribution.

9. Upon asking yourself if the findings are reasonable, your answer is no.

You can be certain that groups of people never do anything erratic or startling; it is the individual who does that. If Queen Isabella had polled her constituents before hocking her jewels, Christopher Columbus never would have sailed. The results of the poll likely would have shown that a majority of people in Spain considered Columbus a lazy foreigner who sat on the dock day after day doing nothing and had a weird notion that the world was round. The majority of Spaniards would have recommended that the queen give no money to Columbus.

If you receive a poll reporting that 66% of the people surveyed say that rattlesnakes are friendly, don't believe it and don't pass it on to your audience. The poll may have been conducted among six snake handlers, four of whom are still alive.

Questionnaires: What You Ask Is What You Get

I know a man who spreads destructive gossip merely by asking a simple question. He would whisper this question in your ear about a person mutually known: "Do you think Charlie has a drinking problem?" That is the surest way to plant the idea that Charlie has a drinking problem without saying so directly. The implication is that he has found reason to ask such a question. Whispering this question in many ears is likely to have many fingers pointing at Charlie.

QUESTIONS WORDED TO DECEIVE

Questions timed and phrased with the intent to deceive can be as destructive as outright lies. Often the intent of a biased question is more easily concealed than a biased statement. Devious propagandists know this and use questions in surveys or polls to enforce their viewpoint.

"Are you getting all the news you need from the Daily Trombone?" Of course not. The Daily Trombone doesn't publish my chess team's scores or my wife's bridge club standings. It doesn't tell me what kind of mood my boss will be in tomorrow when I shall ask him for a raise in pay.

"All," An Unattainable Reference

The Daily Trombone might be doing a fair job of covering the news as newspapers go, but when the word "all" was used, it puts the matter into an unattainable reference — a role that no mass medium could fulfill. Respondents may agree that the newspaper does a good job of reporting most of the news, but they are not likely to accept the idea on an "all" or "always" basis. Politicians sometimes use this logic when challenging incumbents who are defending their record. The President of the United States seems to be a perennial victim of this "all" logic. According to his critics, he does not do "all" he can (or not enough) for the poor, the aged, the environment, and so on.

Respondents Prefer the Status Quo

Generally people are disposed to accept the status quo. Therefore when you notice a question using words such as "as it is now," or other phrases that specify the current condition, it should not surprise you if the response to such a question favors no change.

> *"Television Station WXYZ has been misrepresenting facts for years, do you think it ought to change now?"*

This question will likely get the survey sponsor solid approval to continue misrepresenting.

Prestige Bias

Prestige is another hang-up a sly questionnaire writer uses. Most of us like to impress other people with our wisdom, knowledge, and experience. Propagandists know that respondents prefer to associate with the more socially accepted behavior and disassociate themselves with the less accepted behavior. They use this technique to emphasize their viewpoint.

"What do you think of Carroll O'Connor?"
"You mean the guy who plays Archie Bunker, the racist, in "All In The Family" on Channel 2 Saturday nights?"
"Yes."
"I never watch the show."

"How about the statement made by William Buckley regarding the President's visit to the Near East?"
"You mean on his program?"
"Yes."
"I missed it that week."

Vote for Good/Against Evil

Similarly, there is a tendency for people to vote for the perceived good people and vote against the perceived bad people. Attributing a statement to Benedict Arnold will get you more votes against it than if the same statement were attributed to Billy Graham.

"Pro-abortionists say that the Daily Trombone generally reports the news objectively. Do you agree or disagree?"

The response to this question will be more a measure of the number of pro-abortionists versus anti-abortionists than a measure of the objectivity the newspaper's news coverage.

Abuse of the "Good" Idea

Some questions are more obviously loaded in favor of the good. It didn't take long for the public to catch on. A recent newspaper story reported the public's irritation in response to the following questions asked of a sample of citizens in a survey sponsored by a Midwest State Board of Education.

"If these nations were tested, which nation would you want (name of state) to match?"

- Australia
- Canada
- China
- France
- Great Britain
- Italy
- Japan
- South Korea
- Sweden
- U.S.S.R.
- West Germany
- None. I would want (name of state) to beat them all.

"What should (name of state) high school graduation rate be in the year 2000?"

- 100 percent
- 95 percent
- 90 percent
- 85 percent
- 80 percent
- 75 percent
- 70 percent

"When the survey is conducted in the year 2000, what grade would you want people to give their own local public schools in (name of state)? (Mark one only.)"

- A
- B
- C
- D
- Fail

When the results were released, some people were outraged, calling the survey "self-serving . . . nonsensical and gratuitous . . . Who wouldn't want (name of state) to score highest? . . . No one wants dropouts . . . It was an idiotic questionnaire. I assume it was for political purposes."

Another good versus evil question is this:

"The United States finds itself in a struggle against Saddam Hussein to free the people of Kuwait while preserving a sufficient supply of oil for the world. Do you favor or oppose increased government expenditures for this purpose?"

It would have to be a heartless cur to answer "no" to such a question.

Split the List Bias

Another ploy in creating response bias is to split a list. Reducing response choices will generate higher numbers for each option. Let us say that there are six department stores in your area. Three are in one end of town and the other three are in the other end of town.

> *"Please tell me in which of the following department stores do you prefer to do most of your shopping?"* Store A, Store B, Store C, Store D, Store E, or Store F.

Each store here competes with five other stores. However, by splitting the list, the choices are reduced and percentages are increased substantially.

> *"Please tell me in which of the following* east side *department stores do you prefer to do most of your shopping?"* Store A, Store B, or Store C.

> *"Please tell me in which of the following* west side *department stores do you prefer to do most of your shopping?"* Store D, Store E, or Store F.

Each store is now competing with only two other stores. If all the stores received an equal share from the first question, each store would receive 16.7% of the mentions. From the latter two questions, each store would receive 33% of the mentions.

Designed to Tell More than They Ask

Some questions are designed to tell more than they ask.

> *"How much should the state spend for road construction next year?"* (a) $150 million (b) $155 million (c) $160 million.

It makes little difference which category respondents select. The categories tell the respondents how much the state wants to spend on road construction next year. By making the difference between each category small, the state is telling the public how much it wants to spend. It makes little difference which category the respondents select. Usually respondents have a propensity to avoid extremes. They probably would select the middle value, $155 million, exactly what the state wanted.

Questions Should Provide Direct Opposite Alternatives

Professional researchers are careful to provide alternatives to options that are direct opposites. They feel that not having an alternative creates a bias favoring the stated alternative.

"Do you like ice cream?" is considered to create a bias in favor of a "yes" response. Instead they prefer to ask the question to read, *"Do you like ice cream, or not?"* Are you *"for or against?"* Do you *"agree or disagree?"* The alternative should always be the direct opposite. Question options not containing direct opposite alternatives will lead to confusing responses.

> *"Generally speaking, would you say that most people can be trusted or that you can't be too careful in dealing with people?"*

Selecting either alternative does not oppose the other. What we have here are two questions combined into one. Another example:

> *"Do you like men's white shirts or do you think pink shirts go better with a navy blue suit?"*

Respondent Must Be Capable of Answering the Questions

Obviously, if questionnaire writers use words people do not understand or ask questions on issues with which respondents have no knowledge, it is not likely that respondents can answer the questions intelligently.

"Would you say that Zaire has a communist government, a dictatorship, or a democracy?"

This question is not likely to achieve a high response rate. Some respondents will admit they don't know the answer, whereas others may guess. The response of those who do know will be corrupted by those who guess. Response to this question has little value.

Timing Is Important

Asking a question about an incident occurring many years ago might yield drastically different responses now than it would have when the incident occurred. Much depends on the extent attitudes have changed over the years.

"Do you think the United States made a mistake in dropping the atom bomb on Hiroshima and Nagasaki, or not?"

This question is more likely to get you more agreement now that the United States made a mistake than at the time when the bombs were dropped.

Blatantly Loaded Questions

Sometimes we are exposed to blatantly loaded questions. These are usually easy to detect.

"Do you agree or disagree that the United States should not interfere in the internal affairs of Third World countries?"

This question would yield a resounding "agree" that the United States ought to butt out of the internal affairs of

Third World countries. The word "interfere" is the culprit. If the word "consult," or "assist," or "help" is used, the response might be much different.

SUMMARY

It goes without saying that questions posed to people should be understandable, devoid of bias, and that the people queried should be capable of answering those questions. Bias enters a question when:

- there is little likelihood that the question can be understood;
- words having unattainable ability such as "all," . . . "everything you ever need to know" are used;
- questions inject a prestige factor;
- the status quo is inferred;
- voting for the good is invoked;
- attribute a view to persons or organizations;
- a list of possible responses is divided into several questions;
- alternatives are not directly opposite;
- and when questions are blatantly loaded.

What to Do

As professional journalists on the receiving end of survey reports, we should be critical of survey questions—that is, when they are made available to us. If the issue is important, we should evaluate the question wording. How else can we evaluate the objectivity of the questions?

The first step is to learn who sponsored the survey. Check for a motive. A survey sponsored by a gun control group may show entirely different results than a survey sponsored by an anti-gun control group.

The second step is to answer the questions yourself as though you were a part of the sample. Look for the biases we mentioned in this chapter and those in Chapter 10. If you are satisfied that the questions seem free of bias, the methodology is sound, and the findings make sense, feel comfortable in passing them on to your audience.

Conclusion

Numbers can be made to speak with more emphasis than words. Put numbers and words together and they become powerful convincers.

If I wanted to convince you that we needed a law prohibiting people from raking leaves, I would cite the number of back injuries resulting from that exercise. I would base the argument on straightforward numbers. Assuming that there were 10,000 people with that kind of back injury in the United States last year, I would use that number, instead of a percentage, to convince you to vote for the enactment of a law prohibiting raking of leaves. After all, 10,000 is so much more convincing than .004%; the percent (10,000 injured) is of 250,000,000 people in the United States (10,000 ÷ 250,000,000 × 100 = .004%). To top it off, I would suggest that you invite all the woeful victims for dinner at your house—just in case you might get the idea that 10,000 is not a sufficiently large number.

Conversely, if the numbers show that three of the five people in our neighborhood who were stung by hornets in the past 20 years died from the sting, we could make a good case against hornets. We simply say that 60% of the people in our neighborhood stung by hornets died from the sting. We will just forget to mention the incidents occurred over the past 20 years. Do you think this is deceiving? Read on. It gets better.

We can make our case even more deceptive. We could say that 100% of the people in our neighborhood who were stung by hornets died. We just forget to mention that two died years later from other causes. You may recall from a previous chapter how anti-smoking lobbyists used this technique. They blamed cigarettes for any smoker who died of lung cancer, ignoring all other causes.

This type of statistical sorcery goes on almost every day. It comes to us mainly from the news media because many reporters have not had sufficient training in evaluating numbers, or they cannot devote the necessary time to the numbers because of deadline pressure.

If you are one of those who hates numbers, you might as well learn to like them or you will be fooled every time and thus fool others. Try to be alert to the pitfalls mentioned in the previous chapters. In general, be especially critical when too much emphasis is put on the accuracy of the numbers or the authority of the source. And watch when the number is surrounded by an abundance of scientific jargon. Often the jargon is used to impress you into believing the numbers. There are no numbers that cannot be explained in everyday language, and you don't need to be a mathematician to understand them.

You can become a fair reporter if you just learn the English language. But if you want to be a great reporter, you must master numbers as well as you master words, and then add objectivity to your style. Generally, mass media provide suggested format and style governing the press releases they will accept. Include a paragraph or several paragraphs on how numbers and survey data should be reported.

For *averages,* require to see how the average was calculated, the number of units in the data set (sometimes called *cases*), and the maximum and minimum values. If the average is an arithmetic mean, require that the standard deviation be given.

For *percentages* and *index numbers,* insist on seeing the base number for every percentage reported.

When *survey data* is sent to you, require that the methodology is reported in some detail including the size of the sample, how it was drawn, table of sampling tolerances (each subset of a sample has its own sampling tolerance), who was interviewed, the completion ratio, and the exact wording of the questions.

Be careful to note the various *modifiers* used in connection with numbers and make certain that they express what the numbers mean. For example, any percent above fifty can never be small. It is a majority of the base number from which it was calculated. Conversely, 1% is never large. It could, however, be exceptional in some instances.

Require that *any other numbers* sent to you include how the numbers were calculated, who calculated or arrived at them, and who sponsored the finding of them.

Remember that *probabilities* are averages of events occurring. It requires many attempts before the proportion of occurrences is stabilized. Inherent in averages is dispersion—the range between the smallest number and the largest number in the data set. Some persons look at it as the chance to beat the odds, but if the odds are loaded against them, the more attempts they make, the more they are likely not to make it. If the odds are one in five of getting the boss's job when he retires, one might go for it. But, if the boss has a niece who is also vying for his job, the odds of getting it are reduced substantially, to say the least.

Finally, if you think all of this requires too much work on your part, don't bother. Be content to lead an easy life. You will join many sheep out there who are content to let others do their thinking. On the other hand, if you learn to understand numbers, you will become the one doing the thinking for the others.

The choice is yours. Good luck!

Subject Index